JOB SPA

12 weeks to refresh, refocus, and recommit to your career

Milo Sindell and Thuy Sindell, Ph.D.

authors of *Sink or Swim*

avon, massachusetts

Copyright © 2008 by Milo Sindell and Thuy Sindell
All rights reserved. This book, or parts thereof, may not be reproduced in any form without permission from the publisher; exceptions are made for brief excerpts used in published reviews.

Published by Adams Business
Adams Media, an F+W Publications Company
57 Littlefield Street
Avon, MA 02322
www.adamsmedia.com

ISBN-13: 978-1-59869-473-4
ISBN-10: 1-59869-473-1

Printed in the United States of America.

J I H G F E D C B A

Library of Congress Cataloging-in-Publication Data
is available from the publisher.

This publication is designed to provide accurate and authoritative information with regard to the subject matter covered. It is sold with the understanding that the publisher is not engaged in rendering legal, accounting, or other professional advice. If legal advice or other expert assistance is required, the services of a competent professional person should be sought.

—From a *Declaration of Principles* jointly adopted by a Committee of the American Bar Association and a Committee of Publishers and Associations

Many of the designations used by manufacturers and sellers to distinguish their product are claimed as trademarks. Where those designations appear in this book and Adams Media was aware of a trademark claim, the designations have been printed with initial capital letters.

This book is available at quantity discounts for bulk purchases.
For information, please call 1-800-289-0963.

CONTENTS

Acknowledgments

We would like to thank our parents for their continued love and support. In particular, to Gerry Sindell for your encouragement and guidance. To Michael Snell, we are grateful for your enthusiasm and guidance as our agent.

To the Adams Media team, your support in helping to create a great first book and seeing the potential in our second book is unsurpassed.

Thank you to our professional influences, including Beverly Kaye, Marshall Goldsmith, and Sue Bethanis.

Finally, to our Olde English Bulldogges, Curtis and Charlotte, you are the cutest and smelliest office mates on the planet, but you were always there to cheer us on. Thank you all for your support and accompaniment on another journey to impact the world of work.

a must-read user instruction
WELCOME TO YOUR JOB SPA

Me, me I want more!

—Mike Muir, lead vocals, Suicidal Tendencies

Why spend way too much of your life doing something you don't enjoy? What if the assorted activities you performed between the hours of 8 A.M. and 5 P.M. Monday through Friday became something you actually enjoyed and found fulfillment in doing? Fantasy? We think not. Your job has the potential to be a conduit for your contribution to the world, a venue of discovery, and a pathway to your broader career objectives.

In your hands is your on-the-job refresh and tune-up kit: a twelve-week guide to help you commit to your success. We are not asking you to commit to your job. Instead we are asking you to commit to your success. There is a difference between the two. Balance what you give to your job with what you take in return. Whether you have been in your job for one, five, or ten years, today is the day you begin to get more from what you do.

The next twelve weeks will be a time of reflection and declaration. You will identify what is important to you, what you want from your job beyond a paycheck, what you want to contribute, and a direction for your future. This is your chance to get professionally refreshed and invigorated. *Job Spa* provides you with a plan and the five professional skills required to reinvigorate yourself and to achieve your vision of success.

Take a Cold Plunge

Before we get started, it's important to provide context for why you need to own your career. Over the past forty years, the implied social agreement between employers and employees has changed. Under the old contract employers acted as parental figures and provided employees with a lifetime of structure and support in exchange for hard work and loyalty. Remember those good old days?

Today, employment is "at will." This means you and your services can be terminated at any time. Between the early 1970s and 2000, more than 30 million people were laid off (Louis Uchitelle, *The Disposable American*, New York: Knopf, 2006).

The good news about these changes is that you probably would not want to work for the same company or have the same job over your entire career. The bad news is that the level of employee trust and commitment has eroded. Companies have sent a message, and not surprisingly, employees have responded. According to 2004 Gallup research, more than 70 percent of employees are not engaged with their jobs. "Not engaged" can range from going through the motions at work to completely checking out and looking for a new job.

When employees aren't engaged with their job, companies suffer as a result of high turnover and lost productivity. But before you laugh, declare that it serves them right, and go back to the midmorning Web search for odd news of the day, consider the following: Being unhappy or unsatisfied with your job impacts *you,* too. Unhappy employees are more stressed, find less satisfaction in their job, have fewer friendships at work, and earn less money over the course of their careers. It is in your interest to get engaged and find satisfaction in what you do.

Pause for a moment and think about the last time that you enjoyed what you did at your job. Time went by quickly. You were focused. Maybe you were challenged, and you pushed to think through a solution? You might have even had fun in the process.

Explode the Workplace Myths

Despite the reality of layoffs, employment at will, and corporate survival of the fittest, employees want to cling to old expectations and ideals, which have become workplace myths. Here are the big three myths.

- **MYTH 1** My boss/manager is my mommy or daddy and will take care of me.
  Nope! Your boss/manager is not there to take care of you. If you are lucky, you will have a boss/manager who will provide guidance, support, and maybe has a sense of humor. It's up to you to seek out opportunities, develop your skills, and build your resume.

- **MYTH 2** My hard work will always be recognized and rewarded.
  Sorry! Think again. Do you actually think the CEO will suddenly recognize your years of silent toiling and finally give you the recognition you deserve? In fact, it's up to you to identify and communicate your achievements.

- **MYTH 3** Company loyalty equals job security.
  Denial! You know the stats. You read the headlines. Despite the reality, you want to believe that your loyalty will override the company's need to make the bottom line look good. The truth is that you need to own your career even if it means changing teams.

It's time to pop the bubble and live in reality. *You* own your career. *You* are responsible for setting your own professional goals, developing the right skills, and building your resume. Over the course of your career and in any job, you have two responsibilities:

1. To your company; to do what you were hired to do
2. To yourself; to develop your skills, to create opportunities, and to manage your career

Regardless of whether your company has made clear its expectations of you, you must also take charge and be clear about your expectations of your employer. Beyond a juicy salary and health-insurance benefits, what do you want in exchange for contributing your skills, abilities, and expertise?

What about learning opportunities so you can develop more skills and be more marketable? What about career advancement? What about a positive work environment? You won't get what you want if you don't know what you want. When your expectations are clearly defined, you will be able to provide the maximum value to your company, and they will be able to meet your needs.

This is what your Job Spa is for:

1. To make sure you are giving 100 percent to your job
2. To make sure you are taking 100 percent from your job

Using This Book

Job Spa is not your cheerleader telling you to put a smile on your face and hunker down to find the gold coin in a pile of manure. If you hate your job and you have neither the hope nor the desire to make it better, save yourself some time and misery: Consider quitting. But if you want more from your job and are ready to invest in yourself, then you have the right book.

The objective of *Job Spa* is to help make your current job more fulfilling and help you take charge of your career. Life is too short.

You spend way too much time at work not to be clear on what you want to *give* and *take* from your job. Start your Job Spa experience by making a commitment to your success. Over the next twelve weeks, you will build upon your commitment and exercise critical professional skills that will help you succeed throughout your career.

The remainder of this chapter provides an overview of the five Job Spa skills. Why take the time to read the remainder of the chapter? Like stretching your muscles before your favorite nature hike, it's important to understand a little bit about the five Job Spa skills and *why* they are important before you start your Job Spa. Each chapter will provide you with weekly detailed information about how to apply the Job Spa skills. During the next twelve weeks at work, you will:

- Read only one *Job Spa* chapter per week (Do-able even in the most time-constrained life!).
- Receive guidance on how and when to apply your Job Spa skills on the job as part of your job (Easy!).
- Plan your activities consistently and build momentum toward success (Results!).

Job Spa helps you figure out what steps you need to take each week to get professionally reinvigorated. This includes seeing new opportunities, making a contribution that means something to you, creating your own PR Plan, and strengthening work relationships. Each week builds on the work you did in the previous week. Throughout the next twelve weeks, you will gather information, think about what you are learning, apply it, and continuously fine-tune your Job Spa skills.

The Five Job Spa Skills

The goal of this book is to ensure that you make the most of your potential by renewing your commitment to yourself. The five Job

Spa skills will bring your commitment to fruition. Here's what you will learn:

GOAL What do you want from your job and what do you want to contribute? Commit to your success by setting clear goals. Put a plan in place to get what you want.

TIME Rediscover how to make time work for you. This includes the most important elements of effective time management and how to master them for maximum results.

KNOWLEDGE Be known for your capacity to contribute. Energize your thirst for knowledge, identify the most valuable sources of knowledge to do your job, reinvigorate your network of knowledge resources and the most effective techniques to share what you know with others.

TEAM Make the most of every relationship. Every employee who wants to succeed, whether she is part of a team or works alone, must be a team player. Here we will refresh your understanding of what it means to work well with others to build a lasting network of partnerships.

IMAGE Ensure your hard work pays off. Craft the right professional image. Focus on the skills and subtle intricacies of identifying, creating, and communicating your personal PR plan.

This book is meant not merely to be read, but to be used. As you experience your *Job Spa*, dog-ear the pages, and write down your reactions. Use the calendar section at the end of each chapter to capture your ideas. Soak it in!

The following section goes into detail about the Job Spa skills. These skills may seem obvious or very familiar to you; but knowing is not the same thing as doing. Note: If you have read our book

Sink or Swim, these skill descriptions are going to be familiar and you will still want to refresh yourself before you start your Job Spa treatment.

Goal

Whether you are aware of it, your job holds many promising opportunities. To make the most of them, define what you want. Most of us talk about what we want, but few of us actually achieve our dreams. The reason this happens is that we don't set effective goals.

Effective goals turn desires into reality. When you have clearly defined goals, you no longer sit back and wait for things to happen. Rather, you are an active participant and make things happen. Having clearly defined goals means that every small thing you do builds toward something bigger. Even seemingly mundane tasks have meaning and a larger context. The goals that you set as part of Job Spa will be powerful because they will have personal significance and clearly defined results. Effective goals require that you do the following:

1. Create achievable goals.
2. Commit to your goals.
3. Determine what success looks like.
4. Design the plan to get you to your goal.

Create Achievable Goals

The likelihood of accomplishing your goals is increased when you stick to a few basics:

- Set goals that are realistic and provide a challenge.
- Set goals that do not contradict any of your other goals.
- Set goals that are in your control.
- Set goals that are positive and reflect what you *really* want.

When it comes to your goals, size matters. Be realistic. If you set a goal to end homelessness, it will feel like you are staring up at a cliff. It's a wonderful aspiration and appears to be a daunting task. That doesn't mean you should throw away your goal. Try breaking your big goal down to more manageable chunks, and you may find there are four smaller goals that lead to your bigger goal.

So, let's say you really want to take on homelessness . . . good for you! Start with a smaller goal such as ending homelessness in your community. Then proceed to the state level, and so on. When you define the components that make up your goals, you break even the largest, wildest ambition into manageable pieces. Each component provides a good challenge and fulfilling result.

Your goals also cannot contradict each other. Let's say your goal is to save enough money for early retirement, and you simultaneously want to lease a new Mercedes as a weekend car. These two goals can be tough to reach since they contradict each other. If your goal is to save money, the Mercedes will have to wait.

Set goals that are in your control. Sometimes we establish goals that require or depend upon things we cannot control. You can't push yourself to try your best when you don't have control over the outcome. There will be none of that here! Let's say you want to build a better relationship with a challenging coworker. By setting the goal, "I want grumpy Bob to be more cooperative," you give control to grumpy Bob. You can't make grumpy Bob be more cooperative. The outcome is not in your control, nor does the goal allow you to take ownership of what you need to do in order to succeed.

A goal that is in your control and that would provide a similar outcome is: "I will take the time to build a more productive and positive relationship with Bob." Note the difference: In the description of the second goal, you have identified the steps that you control and can act upon.

Finally, state your objectives and the behavior required in a positive way. For example, the goal "I will not miss my deadlines" emphasizes a current negative behavior: missing deadlines. When you state this goal in the positive, "I will hit my deadlines," you focus on the future, and what you need to do to make this happen. Your words shape a positive direction for your efforts. Your attention is now focused on the good things that you will do differently.

Commit to Your Goals

Now that you know what you want, it is important to understand why you want it. Have you ever wondered why most diets end in disappointment? Although the "what" is clear, the "why' is missing. Most of us set goals that we are not really committed to because we have not confirmed the fundamental reasons why we want to achieve the goal. When you are clear on why you want a particular goal, the goal has a deeper, more personal meaning. You increase the likelihood that you will keep on track even during those times when you may feel overwhelmed or distracted.

Finally, write your goals down. It's amazing how people very quickly forget what they want to achieve. When you write down your goal, it is your second step toward making a commitment so that it turns into a reality. Something very powerful occurs when you transfer an idea into a physical form. You are making a declaration. Review your written goals as a visual reminder. You'd be amazed how real a desired goal becomes when you put it in writing.

Paint the Picture of Success

If you ask someone who has achieved his goals how he did it, you will usually find that he had a way to score his progress. That means he always knew if he was getting closer to his goals, and he was clear on when he achieved his goals. He knew what success looked like.

Define what success looks like for your goals:

- What will be different tomorrow versus where you were today?

- What will you see? What will the finished product look like? Will people be more interested to talk with you? Will you get more invitations to meetings? An award? Recognition from your team?
- What will you hear? How will you talk about your achievement with others? What will people say when you achieve your goal? Will they say they had a positive experience working with you?
- How will you feel? Relieved? Delighted? Excited? Will it have been a positive experience? Will you have worked hard?

It's easier to create a plan once you are clear what your goal is and success looks like. You know exactly which direction you are moving in.

Design the Plan

After you have identified your goals, the next step is to design a plan that will take you to where you have set your sights. An effective plan will be your map. Your plan will include milestones, tasks, time, and resources to reach your goals.

When you develop your plan, focus on these key elements:

- *Milestones:* Identify the major points of your project that must get completed. For example, an early milestone may be that you need to enroll the support of key contributors to your project.
- *Tasks:* Identify the more minute tasks that make up your milestones. For example, to enroll support, you will need to call each person and set a meeting time and date.
- *Time:* Give yourself a realistic time frame for completion of your goal, milestones, and tasks. For example, you have given yourself three months to reach your project goal. Your milestone, to ensure everyone is on board, will take one month. The task of calling each person to set a time to meet can be done within one week.
- *Resources:* Determine the things you need to reach your goal. For example, besides meeting with key contributors to the project,

what other information do you need? What about a budget or additional skills that will be required to complete the project?

Your plan should reflect the simplicity or complexity of your goals. Short-term or smaller goals may only require a task list. Larger goals may require a plan that outlines milestones, tasks, time frames, your existing skills, skills that require development, and resources required for reaching a goal.

Time

Time management seems to be one of those things that everybody needs to do, but few are actually good at. The reality is that good time management is a necessity in the business world. Now, don't run and hide from it just yet. Breathe in. Breathe out. Relax! It'll be fine. *Job Spa* will help you learn—painlessly—how to be a great time manager one easy step at a time. You'll learn to focus on the planning process, how to be realistic in allotting the appropriate amount of time to each task, and how to stick to your schedule.

Time management is not just about meeting deadlines and showing up for work on time. Effective time-management skills demonstrate to others that you are a winner: focused, reliable, consistent, and professional. Time-management skills will also help you balance work's daily demands and give you time to achieve additional aspirations.

Plan Wisely

Good planning is the secret to successfully managing your time. Planning means you regularly think ahead to choose exactly what you want to accomplish and allocate the appropriate amount of time amid all the distractions and interruptions of the workday. Take five minutes at the beginning of every week to plan for the week ahead.

As part of this planning process, create and/or review your task list. It does not take much time, but it does take discipline. The reward? Your priorities will snap into focus. You will always know where you are in your day and what you can accomplish.

Managing your time does not mean that you can always control your time. The unexpected will happen. Allow room for surprises. To better cope with unpredictability, control the way your day starts off. Begin your morning with a routine that gives you the opportunity to seize the day. The magic of the right morning routine is that you start off ready and prepared for whatever comes your way. Your routine provides you with predictability in a chaotic world.

Allocate Time Effectively

Most task lists and planning fall apart because people don't give themselves enough time to complete the job. Can you think of a time when you thought you'd get something done in two hours and found it really took four? Can you see anything in particular that caused you to run long? Life and work are full of distractions. Maybe someone popped in for a quick chat; maybe you had a meeting that ran over. And there are always the usual delays: heavy traffic, urgent e-mails, computer crashes, and unexpected phone calls.

As interruptions surface, you are often expected to respond ASAP. That's why you need to create a time buffer if you're going to stick to your daily plan. This means creating enough leeway to complete tasks—despite the inevitable distractions and interruptions. Be realistic and accurate when you schedule events. Even the most savvy time manager plans for interruptions. Set yourself up for success.

Track and Keep to Your Schedule

Let's imagine that you have planned realistically and given yourself enough time to complete your projects. Great! Now, for the last piece of the puzzle: keeping track of your schedule. Have you ever had the experience of getting into what seemed like a brief conversation, and it was so interesting that you lost track of time? Now imagine that happening as you're dashing from one meeting to another. It is guaranteed that people are going to stop you in the hallway or poke their heads into your cubicle or office for a quick question. Some of these interruptions are going to be important, and some are going to be time suckers. Bottom line: They are all going to be distracting. Added together, these little special moments take a big bite out of your schedule!

What to do? When you get sidetracked or interrupted, be aware of how much time is ticking away. Take that five, seven, or ten minutes into account *while it's happening*. This means thinking, "Hmmm . . . five minutes already, and Carol is still talkin' about her cat's new diet program. All I want is a status on the numbers." If the matter is urgent, politely interrupt and let Carol know that you are really glad that Mr. Cuddles is regular again and you want to continue the conversation over lunch. "Carol, I can see this is important and I want to hear the whole story. I'm on a killer deadline. Can we catch up on this later?" People will understand. If it turns out to be important, you'll hear the whole story. If it turns out Carol just needed to chat or vent, you've only lost five minutes of your time because you stopped her. Otherwise, you would've lost twenty minutes and gotten way too much information on Mr. Cuddles. Manage interruptions to avoid priority derailment. Additionally, use the following tools and strategies to manage your time:

- *Use a calendar:* Plan your days and weeks. Mark out time for your meetings, project work, and other events on a weekly basis. Include a time buffer for potential surprises, distractions, and other unknowns.
- *Set priorities:* Rate your tasks, and identify what you need to do immediately, soon, and later.
- *Use technology:* Get a digital watch, phone, or electronic calendaring system that uses an alarm to remind you of important appointments.

- *Plan travel time:* Give yourself enough time to get to those appointments and arrive on time. It's always better to arrive ten minutes early than ten minutes late.
- *Work backward:* If you have to be somewhere by a certain time, work backward to ensure having enough time to walk to your next meeting.
- *Focus:* Keep your attention on the task at hand.
- *Finish:* Complete what you set out to do.
- *Commit yourself:* Set aside blocks of time in your calendar to accomplish specific tasks.

Knowledge

When you have the right information, you are able to make the right decisions about what you want from your job, what you have to contribute, and what skills or knowledge you want to develop. Knowledge will be a very important skill during your Job Spa. Explore what you know, what you have to share with your coworkers and company, and identify what new knowledge you want to develop. Use your knowledge to ask even better questions, make more informed decisions, and add value to your team and company. Over the next twelve weeks, identify, develop, and strategically deploy your knowledge in the following areas:

1. Your company
2. Your company's industry
3. Your specific role, job responsibilities, and additional knowledge

Know Your Company

Company knowledge is the information that's unique to your company. This includes its history, culture (why the company does things a certain way), internal operations, strategy, and market share.

When you have company knowledge, you have insight into how your company is organized, how various departments work together, and why there are certain rules and ways of doing things. It can be easy to take this information for granted. However, your understanding of your company is an opportunity.

Over the next twelve weeks, you are going to observe and define your company's culture in a way that you have not done before. You are going to make explicit various methods, values, behaviors, and idiosyncrasies that you previously took for granted. Use this intelligence to craft your plan and shape your behavior for maximum results.

You Are an Industry Expert

Having a strong command of your industry knowledge means that you're looking at the entire business environment that surrounds and influences your company. For instance, if you work for a software company, use your knowledge of the software industry to identify existing and new opportunities. If you work for a clothing company, leverage your understanding of the fashion and retail industries.

No matter how many years of experience you have, it is critical to career success to continually refresh your understanding of the big picture. This helps you make more informed decisions. When you understand your industry, its trends and practices, and how your company fits, you can more effectively see where your job fits, where you can make an impact, and create new opportunities. Seeing the bigger picture keeps you in the driver's seat to make your own career changes as opposed to having the changes made to you.

Define Your Skills

An important component of the knowledge you bring to your job is having what we call subject-matter knowledge. This is the area in which you have expertise or experience. If you are an accountant, you have knowledge of tax laws. If you are in sales, you have expertise in closing a deal. By having subject-matter expertise, you are able to ask insightful questions, make informed recommendations and decisions, and contribute your value to the company.

Treat your knowledge as an evolving resource that you use and share with others. There are three methods for maximizing and managing this resource: Identify areas or subjects you are knowledgeable in, share what you know with others, and identify areas that you want or need to learn more about.

A helpful method to begin to identify what you know is to define your knowledge using these four categories:

1. *Interpersonal knowledge:* An understanding of effective communication skills, relationship dynamics, and knowing how to work with different personality types
2. *Professional knowledge:* Areas that correlate to a specific profession, training, or educational background that relates to your work
3. *Special interest:* Hobbies, education, or research
4. *General knowledge:* A variety of disciplines such as politics, history, cultures, languages, economics, and the arts

Over the next twelve weeks, leverage what you know by identifying your unique strengths and what you want to contribute. The result may be new ideas and opportunities for different ways of doing things. Balance what you have to contribute with what you think your company is actually open to accepting. As you have probably experienced, your company has its own way of adapting to change and adopting new ideas. Consider the right strategy to introduce your ideas in a way that gets support; whether it's a new project proposal to your manager or a broader initiative that may involve an entire division. When you share your knowledge, it ensures you make a contribution, builds your credibility, and expands your network of relationships with coworkers.

Team

Shy, love being in a crowd, collaborating, or working alone; whatever the case, embracing your new Job Spa perspective means successfully coexisting with others. A big part of your Job Spa will focus on strengthening and growing the relationships with your coworkers. So whether you are the pillar of collaboration or the office introvert, it's time to strengthen your relationships and demonstrate your team-player skills.

When you get along well with others, work is easier, you feel inspired, and the creative juices flow. From a purely practical perspective, credible and trusting relationships help you get things done. Are you considered a jerk, or do people like working with you? Take a litmus test:

- Does your team make decisions without you?
- Does your team support you in your decisions or go to bat for you?
- Do you seem to be the last one to find out about things?

Being a team player is about having an attitude and exhibiting a set of behaviors regardless of whether you are part of a close-knit team that interacts regularly on projects or if you work independently. Work well with others even if you have an aversion to the *T* word. Embracing your inner team player means focusing on two critical skills: collaboration and coaching.

Collaboration as Caring and Sharing

Collaboration is about involving other people. Your company is made up of different groupings of people. Depending on their size, these groupings might be referred to as divisions, departments, or teams. As you know, company success depends on the ability of these groups to work together. Each department relies on others to deliver what is required. On a smaller scale, your ability to do your job well also means you need to collaborate. The more you invest in helping others succeed, the stronger the relationships you develop. Thus, the easier it becomes to call upon coworkers in the future. Collaboration can take on many different forms, from getting a coworker's opinion on your ideas to volunteering for a new project team.

In certain situations, working alone gets the job done faster. Sometimes true success involves others in the planning and decision-making stages. Simply asking your coworkers for their input on one of your projects or ideas can create a sense of collaboration and demonstrates to others that you are inclusive—a team player.

Be a Coach

Coaching is about helping other people. A great way to contribute your knowledge, skills, or other resources is through coaching. Yes, you can be a coach! Your first step to coaching is having the right attitude. Are you willing to help? There are many opportunities to act as a coach. As you collaborate on projects, identify what you could teach that would be helpful to others.

A very important part of coaching is being approachable. Your coworkers want to know that they can come to you if they need help or have a question. Sometimes beginning a coaching conversation is as simple as asking others how you can help. Coaching others demonstrates that you are generous enough to invest your time and knowledge in others.

Image

Top leadership consultant Marshall Goldsmith explains that professional image is critical to success, as opposed to being political or self-promotional. "I use the analogy of a Broadway play. The actors are always 'up and positive.' They dress in a certain way. It doesn't matter how they feel. They are not there for themselves. They are there for their customers. Even though they may have done the same play a thousand times, this is the first time this customer has seen it. When I teach people how to change behavior, one of their concerns is being 'phony.' This concern tends to disappear when I ask them to focus on being 'professional.'"

Goldsmith offers a powerful metaphor. The cast and crew do everything possible every single night to present the best show possible. There are no excuses; even though there are always personal problems: dinner last night made me sick, I had a hard time getting a sitter, the subway was running late. In a professional show, none of these excuses are ever even mentioned. *Your* audience is the people in your company. They expect your highest level of performance every day. No excuses. Similarly, you owe it to yourself to be focused and prepared so you can take advantage of opportunities. The right professional image requires you to sharpen and deploy specific interpersonal skills. Develop a strong professional image by doing the following:

1. *Networking:* Get to know others and thoughtfully build your network of contacts.
2. *Communication:* Always be clear and concise in your message, and professional in your tone.
3. *Personal PR:* Send a clear message about what is important to you by developing a personal public relations message that communicates your image and values.

No matter what you know, no matter how good or capable you think you are at getting the job done, your ability to communicate and present yourself as a professional is crucial to your success.

Network

The results you get from networking depend on the investment you make. Successful networking is more than just making contact and expecting rewards for your effort. Networking is about building relationships. Relationships take nurturing. Make the effort to reconnect with your coworkers. Strengthening a network expands the information pipeline and helps you get things done. When people have a need or exciting ideas or projects, they will think of you. You will be included and opportunities will present themselves.

Communicate

How many times have you heard the "good communication skills" song and dance? You know . . . the job requirements that stated good communication skills are a must. Are they really that important? Yes. Do most people do a good job of it? No. Don't take your communication skills for granted. As part of your Job Spa, you will take a step back, evaluate, and deploy communication skills that will drive further success. Effective communication skills are what you say and how you say it: your verbal and nonverbal communication.

What You Say

Effective communication skills help you build relationships, get the resources you need, and give your coworkers confidence in you.

Strong communication skills include the abilities to:

- *Listen and understand:* Stay quiet, do not interrupt, and paraphrase what you heard.
- *Make distinctions:* Ask insightful questions to understand and confirm what the other person is trying to say.
- *Make requests:* Get clear on what you want and ask for it.
- *Communicate information or opinions:* Directly communicate your recommendations and suggestions.

When you effectively apply these communication techniques, you clearly convey your message and better understand the needs of others.

Here are some examples of these skills in action:

- *For your listening skills, here's an example of paraphrasing:* "So what you're saying here is that we need to address customer needs, right?"
- *For making distinctions, here's an example of getting clearer understanding and confirmation:* "When you say 'Customer,' do you mean our internal or external customer, or both?"
- *For making a request, here's an example asking for what you need:* "So we've discussed needing to get a budget completed. May I have your draft by Thursday afternoon?"
- *For communicating information or opinions, here's an example of stating your opinion:* "I agree with your recommendation, and before we commit, I have one concern I'd like to share . . ."

How You Say It

Effective nonverbal communication is as important as verbal communication. Nonverbal communication can reinforce what you are verbally communicating, or unintentionally send a conflicting message. For example, when you say "Great idea," and your arms are crossed and brows furrowed, you send a very different message than when you say it and lean forward with a smile. Regularly ask yourself, "What message is my body language sending, and does it reflect what I am verbally communicating?"

It is also important to notice other people's body language and tone. Is someone using sarcasm to be funny or not taking your ideas seriously? Does a furrowed brow mean the other person does not understand or does not like your ideas? If you notice unfavorable body postures when you are speaking, give your coworkers an opportunity to ask questions. Do not ignore their signals. Acknowledging their body language by saying, "I notice that you are furrowing your brows, I'm wondering if perhaps I am not being clear . . ." demonstrates that you are listening and paying attention to them. It also allows you the opportunity to address any confusion or concerns.

Craft a Personal PR Plan

How do you know that BMW is considered the "ultimate driving machine" when not everyone has owned one? How do you know that Volvo has a great safety record when not everyone has owned one? Through marketing, of course! A word, a picture, and/or a positive anecdote has been associated with an object and been seen or heard by millions of people who have never experienced the product for themselves. When the sales slogan is believed to be true regardless of firsthand experience, that's good marketing!

You, too, have a product to market: yourself. You may not have an advertising budget, but you are still responsible for promoting and managing your image. This is your personal public relations (PR) campaign. With every contact, whether it's a phone conversation, presentation, or meeting, you are presenting an impression of who you are. Your effectiveness and success depend on how you are perceived. You have the opportunity to intentionally redefine yourself. If you aren't explicit about who you are and what you stand for, others will make assumptions and paint the picture for themselves. The intent of your PR message is to communicate your *values* and what you want to be known for to a broader audience.

To create your professional image, determine what is important to you and what you want others to know about you. Next, demonstrate those values with the right behavior. Your words, actions, and look should all be aligned to support the image you want to project.

Craft and launch your personal PR campaign. Every interaction delivers a message and confirms others' perception of you. Put your personal PR message into a plan. Your personal PR plan is composed of three easy steps: say it, show it, and do it.

1. *Say it:* Identify what is important to you. Find a couple of key words or a phrase that captures your values and share it with others consistently.
2. *Show it:* Get taken seriously as a professional by dressing the part. "But I *am* rock 'n' roll and I love my band T-shirts" . . . that's

nice. The only problem is that you happen to work in a conservative accounting firm. Every company has a uniform, whether it's a suit-and-tie law office or a jeans–and–polo shirt computer hardware manufacturer. Know your organization's uniform. Better still, identify the uniform of your company's leaders. If you want to be a future leader in the company, dress the part.

3. *Do it*: Act in a manner that is consistent with what you are saying and showing. If you tell people that it's important that meetings start on time, be there on time or even five minutes early. Your behaviors reinforce your personal PR plan.

Remember: Say it, show it, and do it.

Put It All Together

Now that you've been introduced to the five Job Spa skills, the next step is to start your regime. What follows is a twelve-week guide to build professional skills, get refreshed, and explore new paths. Read one chapter per week. Each week has a theme. There will be specific goals to accomplish, skills to practice, and questions to ponder. *Job Spa* also provides suggestions for specific actions as well as reminders for what you should be doing each week with respect to the five Job Spa skills.

Keep in mind that the pace of your company may require that you speed up or slow down how you apply the content presented in the following chapters. This is your guide and a resource to help you succeed. Make it work for you.

A Final Note

These next twelve weeks in your job are an important time in your life. You will want to take extra care that you are minimizing outside distractions and ensure that you are setting yourself up for success.

Give yourself every opportunity to succeed and enjoy your Job Spa. For instance, consider holding off signing up for that night art class. If you normally stay out late during the week, you might want to change your routine and make sure you're getting lots of rest. This is your time and your opportunity. Give yourself every chance to dig deep, learn, and get refreshed!

week one
CHOOSE YOUR SUCCESS

"Hi, my name is Charlie. I have been with my current employer for almost four years. During this time I have changed jobs a couple of times, and luckily these changes have worked out. The first change was the result of a new company initiative that my manager led. The second change was the result of a reorganization of the company. That was a pretty nerve-racking time. We knew changes were going to take place, including layoffs. The whole department went into this strange mood. Luckily when the dust finally settled I still had a job—albeit a different one.

"If someone asked me how I see myself and my career, the word that pops up is 'passive.' I do my job—it's fine, but that's it. At the same time I find myself bored. I want to be excited. I want to be interested in my job. I don't think my company gets that I have a lot to offer. Admittedly, I haven't taken extra initiative either because I am still not clear on what is in it for me."

Welcome to Week One!

Job Spa is your opportunity to review, refresh, and get focused on what you want and need to do in order to triumph at work. Over the next twelve weeks, give yourself an opportunity that few people allow themselves. Focus on *yourself* and *your* success at work. The great thing about Job Spa is that your spa experience takes place on the job as part of your job.

Why take a Job Spa? Let's think about the stats. You spend eight hours a day at work (if not more). That means you spend at least a third of your adult lifetime working. That's a significant amount of time. Why not make the most of it? Starting in the 1950s, research and variations of this initial research on the meaning of work posed the question: "Would you stop working if you won the lottery or inherited a substantial amount of money?" Over the course of time and even during shifts of social influences, more than 70 percent of people still state that they would continue working (R. Snir and I. Harpaz. "To Work or Not to Work: Non-Financial Employment Commitment and the Social Desirability Bias," *Journal of Social Psychology*, 2002, pp. 635–644). Surprisingly, according to a 2004 Gallup poll, more than 70 percent of people are disengaged from their job. This disconnect between data underlies the tension that most of us have between the desire to draw fulfillment from our jobs and the challenges to achieving that fulfillment.

WE'RE NOT ASKING you to turn off reality and pretend that everything in your work is or can be perfect. We are asking that you make a choice to shift your attitude, get clear on what you want, and change what you give and get from your work. You can continue to whine, snivel, and complain, or you can actually do something that will make a substantial difference in your life.

Despite the significance that our jobs play in our lives, most people spend their professional lives meandering from job to job, experience one or multiple careers, and, if they are lucky, end up someplace they want to be. The rewards are too great and the consequences too dire to leave professional fulfillment to luck. Moving from luck to taking action requires choosing to commit to your success. Committing to your success will help you get re-energized about existing work and help you see the potential in yet-to-be identified opportunities. This is your chance to significantly change how you perceive your job and future.

How to Use This Book

Job Spa follows a week-by-week process for taking the right actions, developing skills, and getting what you want from your job. The skills that you will focus on deploying are universal to professional success. You may believe you already know and do these skills. Whether you are new to your career or a veteran, we challenge you to further improve your skills. Let's be honest, you may know these skills, but do you *do* them, do them *well*, and do them *consistently*?

Read one chapter each week, and practice and apply what you are learning on the job as part of your job. At the end of each section are Job Spa Bonus Challenges to help you apply what you are reading.

Friendly word of advice: If you are not ready to commit to your success, then you will need to reschedule your Job Spa. Like any important decision, getting the most from your Job Spa requires making the commitment and sticking to it. Are you are ready at this time to commit to your success? This commitment will be the foundation for your perspective, attitude, and behaviors over the next twelve weeks. *Job Spa* will support and guide you to practice new skills and behaviors that will take you on the path to professional renewal.

WEEK 1	JOB SPA REGIMEN: YOUR 100 PERCENT COMMITMENT
GOALS	Make the commitment.
TIME	Make time for your success.
KNOWLEDGE	Identify what makes you unique.
TEAM	It takes a team.
IMAGE	Take a look in the mirror.

Goal

It's time to start your Job Spa treatment. When you go to a spa, get a professional massage, or enjoy any pampering experience, your objective is very clear: taking care of yourself. Job Spa is no different. You are here to take care of Number One. The first step is to commit to your success by getting what you want and deserve from your work, company, and career. Remember those three workplace myths mentioned in the introduction?

> **MYTH 1** My boss/manager is my mommy or daddy and will take care of me.
> **MYTH 2** My hard work will always get recognized and rewarded.
> **MYTH 3** Company loyalty equals job security.

Popping these myths and getting real about your success is the essence of what Job Spa is all about—*you*! This goal section provides an overview of the most important objective of your Job Spa treatment.

Jump In

The first step is to make the choice and set the goal to get engaged with your job. Here's our challenge to you: For the next twelve weeks, test out a new perspective. This might be easy or challenging, depending on your work environment, history, or outlook. Whatever the case, in order to make the most of your Job Spa, you will need to let go of what might be holding you back and take on a new angle. This is your time and opportunity for change. To make the most of this opportunity, you will need to be completely present, open-minded, and focused on your success. Engagement means you

> **WE'RE NOT ASKING** you to commit 100 percent to your company. We are asking you to commit to your success. This is different.

will walk down the corporate hallways with the following attitude: "I am 100 percent committed to my success." When you make this attitude shift, you start to see your work differently and the opportunities within it. You are intentionally crossing a threshold by making this commitment. Here's what this means:

- You hold yourself to a standard of personal accountability. Don't blame others and make excuses.
- You think big and allow yourself to imagine the possibilities. Don't limit yourself or let history, the recording in your head, or what others say stop you.

Assess your attitude in these areas. In what ways does your attitude need to shift in order to commit to your success? No more looking back. Starting from this point, you are the role model for 100 Percent Commitment to your success.

Attitude is Not Everything

The right attitude is the foundation for the right behaviors. Now that your old attitude has been exfoliated revealing a fresh commitment, let's make sure your behaviors reinforce your new glow. Over the next twelve weeks, try the following set of behaviors on for size:

Give 100 percent to your job
Take 100 percent from your job = *Your 100 Percent Commitment*

Giving 100 percent to your job means that you are committed to giving as much as you can to your job. The behaviors that embody giving 100 percent can take many forms: making your current projects an even bigger success, taking extra initiative, reaching out to coworkers, looking for opportunities to improve your performance, or initiating new projects. Discover what giving 100 percent means to you.

Taking 100 percent from your job requires that you are clear on what you need in return for what you give. Beyond a paycheck and benefits, define what you need in return for your hard work. This might include building skills, establishing greater work/life balance, or perhaps a promotion. What kinds of projects would you like to work on? What kind of relationships do you want to have with coworkers? What opportunities would be fun and stimulating if you were to partner with another function in your company? Do you need more flexible work hours? Discover what taking 100 percent means to you.

Listed in the following chart are examples of giving and taking from your job. Consider how much you currently give and what you currently take. Determine what you need to do to create equity.

YOUR 100 PERCENT COMMITMENT	
GIVE 100 PERCENT	**TAKE 100 PERCENT**
Your attention (be present)	Appropriate salary and benefits
Your strategic thinking skills	Appropriate job title
Your knowledge and perspective	Career development opportunities
Your insights on what can be improved or new opportunities	Stimulating work or projects
Positive and constructive attitude toward coworkers and the company (even if you may not agree with them)	Opportunities to learn new skills
Take initiative and look for opportunities to change or role-model what you don't like about your company or environment (as opposed to complain)	Opportunities to learn from coworkers
Follow through on commitments	Build relationships
Execute work on time and with top quality	Opportunities to travel
Give the appropriate amount of time to your job	Opportunities to try a new role

Your 100 Percent Commitment will help you focus and get more satisfaction from your job. Your 100 Percent Commitment also means that you learn as much as you can, build your resume with experiences, and look for opportunities that promote your success and achieve your goals.

There may be days ahead when your commitment to your success and your undying positive energy are not at the forefront of your mind. Reference the chart, and make note of the behaviors you want to demonstrate over the next twelve weeks—specifically, what you want to give and take. Write down your goals to keep focused. This is the first step to making your goals a reality. The experience of writing a goal down brings your words into physical form. By seeing your words, you cement your commitment.

Let's take it one step further. Write it down *and* post it in several different places. At home, post your message on your bedroom mirror. At work, write a cryptic note to yourself or draw an icon (so the whole world doesn't have to know what you are doing) and put it on your computer monitor and/or on your notebook. These will be visual reminders of your 100 Percent Commitment to your success. These reminders will also keep you focused on those days when you don't feel so hot.

Professional Legacy

Coinciding with your 100 Percent Commitment, it is helpful to consider the big picture: What is the professional legacy you want to build? A professional legacy is the combination of intentional impact that you want to create in each of your jobs and the experience you want to take with you. Your professional legacy can take many forms such as the creation of a new program, mentoring or teaching others, or finding and implementing a better way of doing something.

Understanding the professional legacy you want to create will help strengthen your commitment and clarify your Job Spa goals. Knowing the legacy that you want to create in your company provides focus and motivation.Your work has a fundamentally deeper meaning because you are clear on how it relates to what you want to create. Define and create your professional legacy to reflect what is unique about who you are, what you know, what you want to be known for, and how you want to be remembered.

JOB SPA BONUS CHALLENGE

Write down your 100 Percent Commitment Equation for what you want to give and what you want to take.

Time

Gleaning as much as you can from your Job Spa requires that you take a closer look at how you currently exercise your time skills. Most important, the next twelve weeks will require that you make time for your success. Clear the distractions and make way for the new you.

Time Is on Your Side

Your Job Spa program requires focus. Effectively manage your time so you can focus. In order to support your 100 Percent Commitment, take an inventory of your at-work and outside-work activities.

Boot those that no longer support your trajectory. While success starts with the right attitude, it can be easily thwarted when there are too many distractions. Purge excess distractions or put them aside while you are going through your Job Spa.

We only have so much time and capacity. In your time away from work, consider spending less time watching homemade stunt videos on the Web, searching obscure blogs on lint collection techniques, and even ending the psychology experiment called "being friends with your ex." Take care of yourself. Get enough sleep. Maintain that exercise regime. Eat foods that will give you nourishment and energy.

Give yourself every opportunity to stay focused in the next twelve weeks on your career success. Or not. You may find yourself destitute on a dirty, windswept street corner scratching your unwashed scalp and wishing you had taken that *Job Spa* book more seriously. Do you really want to risk it? We didn't think so.

On the job, identify activities that waste your time (aside from all those staff and project meetings that keep showing up on your calendar) and actions that can maximize your time. You're probably thinking, "But it's all a waste of time." Now, now, we've all been there before: contemplating the meaning of fingernails as John and Sharon from accounting regale you with their Sarbanes-Oxley compliance triumphs on a three-hour conference call. Think about how much time you can maximize by taking the initiative to create meeting agendas, sticking to the agenda and time frame, prioritizing what work needs to get done immediately, and staying focused.

Beginning in this first week, create and maintain a strict calendar and task list. If you already do this, fantastic! Prioritize your existing work and manage your calendar with the discipline of a nun. Seriously, you will want to make sure that you are making time to not only read this book but also work through the various activities that go along with achieving Job Spa success. The things you will be doing as part of your Job Spa experience should already be part of your job. Only now, you are doing these things because they have more significance. They directly support your 100 Percent Commitment.

JOB SPA BONUS CHALLENGE

Name the one thing that you will do to create more time for your Job Spa success.

Knowledge

As mentioned, half of the commitment you will make as part of your Job Spa is defining what you want to contribute to your job. Committing to your success requires more than good intentions. It requires understanding the skills, knowledge, perspectives, and experiences you contribute to your team and company. In order to give 100 percent to your job, you must know what you are capable of giving.

Me, Me, Me

It's all about you! However, your coworkers seem to miss this very important point. Do they know what you can and do contribute? If they don't (because you are not one to boast), here's your opportunity to get clear on why you are amazing.

The first step to making your contribution is defining your knowledge, skills, and perspective. Think of your knowledge as your set of corporate fingerprints. No matter your age, education, or years in your profession, you have a combination of knowledge and perspective that is unique. Most of us take for granted the plethora of information that resides in our heads. It is easy to be unaware of what you know. It is time to look at what is really going on in that great big brain of yours. Start by reviewing the following five questions:

1. *Skills:* What am I good at?
2. *Knowledge:* What do I know (education, training, experience, etc.)?
3. *Resource:* When and why do people come to me for information?
4. *Perspective:* What makes my perspective unique from others?
5. *Personality:* What are my unique personality traits that differentiate me (amiable, responsible, small ego, etc.)?

Ask yourself these questions, and let them marinate for a while. Some answers may come quickly, and others will take more time. Even if you are relatively new to your profession, you still have a unique perspective that sets you apart from everyone else. Understand the knowledge and skills you have to effectively give and take 100 percent.

JOB SPA BONUS CHALLENGE

Create a personal knowledge list based on the five questions.

Team

Team player . . . so you've heard the term a million times. It might even be posted on the conference room walls, put in your evaluation, or even on your security access badge. It's often talked about and rarely witnessed. The elusive team player is a difficult species to track. Every corporate handbook talks about how important it is to be a team player. In reality the team player ethos rarely manifests itself in a consistent manner. Luckily with the help of your Job Spa, you are going to change all that. You are going to become a world-class team player.

Before you roll your eyes and begin to feel woozy, consider the following: Being a team player is a perfect expression of your 100 Percent Commitment: to give as much as you can and take as much as you can. Being a team player is actually quite easy; just think collaboration, make group or project objectives a priority, and look for ways to help your coworkers. Don't worry, there is no need to carry a set of pom-poms and recite the company cheer at the start of every meeting. Being a team player is quite simply an attitude and set of behaviors that make collaboration a reality.

Your team player attitude also forms the basis for whether someone wants to work with you. The laws of reciprocity state that if you are not a team player, you will not likely encounter other team players. You can't make the most of your job by being a pariah. Wouldn't it be great if your reputation as a team player spread throughout the company? Imagine being so popular and in demand that you could cherry-pick your projects.

Team Player Skills in Action

Let's say at your next staff meeting big Bob gives a project status report. You observe that Bob is missing some data that you just so happen to have. Which one of the following do you do?

1. Lean back, smile to yourself, and think, "How could Bob miss such obvious information?" (Tempting, but not team player-esque.)
2. Ask Bob a question that highlights the fact that he missed this data. (Sure, if you wanted to practice your grilling techniques and watch big Bob sweat.)
3. Let Bob know that you think you have some information that can help his project. (Yes, put aside your sadistic musings and throw Bob a bone. You'll feel happy, he'll appreciate your help, and your coworkers will think you're not such a jerk after all.)

If you picked number 3, you are well on your way!

There are two main components of being a team player: collaboration and coaching. Collaboration entails working well with others, understanding shared needs and objectives, and working to ensure that everyone succeeds. Coaching involves helping others by providing your specific knowledge, insight, or expertise.

Later chapters present more information and instructions on how and when to practice these skills. In the meantime, notice where there are opportunities to step up. If you're not willing to contribute and lend a helping hand, you are not committed to your own success. Remember the laws of reciprocity, if your team succeeds, you succeed.

JOB SPA BONUS CHALLENGE

Identify your favorite team experience and what you learned.

Image

Welcome to your first visit to your Image Salon. Before deciding between aromatherapy, shiatsu, or psychotically deep-tissue massage from Olga the weightlifter, you will probably consider the location and level of your aches and pains. Similarly, start your Job Spa by diagnosing specific areas of *professional* aches and pains. Effective diagnosis involves gathering observations from your manager and a few trusted coworkers.

Reality: It's Not Just for Breakfast Anymore

Let's end this ongoing debate about reality versus perception once and for all. It doesn't matter if it's just someone else's perception. For that person, that perception is their reality. To support the shifts you want to make as part of your Job Spa, ask, "How do others really experience me?" As part of committing to your success, we asked you to gauge your own perception of how you give and take 100 percent. Now it's time to compare your perception with those of others.

To ensure you are on the right track to success, it is important to determine how much of your perception is aligned with that of your manager and coworkers. It's easy to go through the motions of work without realizing how others perceive you. You will not be able to make the most of your workplace if your perception is out of whack. Professional fulfillment will be elusive if you think you have expert communication skills, get your work done early, and deliver quality results, when others think that you don't communicate clearly, hand in your work late, and leave out important details in your projects and assignments. As you set your sights on success, confirm with others that your self-perception matches theirs. The best way to ascertain this information is to ask for feedback.

Let Me Give You Some Feedback

Like a dunk into the cold pool after sitting in a steamy sauna, feedback can be quite a rush. No matter how you feel about receiving and giving feedback, this information is critical to your development and long-term success. Feedback is also imperative to starting and making the most of your Job Spa experience.

Keep in mind that asking for feedback does not need to be like formal psychological analysis. You are not asking for information from your coworkers on why they think your mom stopped mashing your carrots when you were three years old or what they think of your moth collection. Your objective is to shine the light on your workplace reality and identify the opportunities to align how you want to be perceived with how others perceive you. Keep it professional, workplace focused, and constructive.

Who and What to Ask

Center your query on two key audiences: Your boss and two or three trusted colleagues. Focus your inquiry on the following areas: your 100 Percent Commitment and your Job Spa skills. Gather your feedback either in person or over the phone. You will want the opportunity to ask for clarification or explore additional questions. Use these questions to start your conversation or create your own:

100 PERCENT COMMITMENT QUESTIONS:

1. *Attitude:* What is your experience of my attitude at work?
2. *Give:* How am I currently contributing to the team and company? How do you think I can contribute more to the team or company?
3. *Take:* Am I making the most of the opportunities around me? Is there anything I should speak up and ask for that I have not articulated?

JOB SPA SKILL QUESTIONS:

1. *Goals:* Do I set effective and realistic goals?
2. *Time:* Do I deliver my projects on time? Effectively manage my time?
3. *Knowledge:* Do I effectively contribute what I know? Am I open to learning?
4. *Team Player:* Do others like to collaborate with me? Am I helpful to others?
5. *Image:* What is my reputation in the department? Do I effectively communicate? Am I seen as professional?

Ask these questions, and get straight answers. This information is critical to building a foundation for your success in the land of reality. If people ask why you are gathering this information, let them know you are starting a book called *Job Spa* that is helping you get professionally refreshed. Gathering their input is part of the beginning steps.

Feedback from Your Manager

Aside from the fact that your manager is your world-of-work higher power, he or she has probably been watching you. Your manager can provide beneficial insight on your performance and what you can do to improve your game. Even if your manager has not been amazingly attentive, she still holds the keys to your success come review time. Asking your manager for feedback communicates that you take your job and career seriously.

Getting feedback does not have to be a big scary process. Your standing meeting with your manager is the perfect setting in which to gather this information. If you don't have regularly scheduled meetings, set up some time for the conversation. This meeting is important to start your Job Spa off on the right foot. Make it a priority. Keep the conversation as informal as needed. This is not your annual review conversation. You can simply say that you have been thinking about your job and you are interested in making sure that you are doing everything that you can to be successful in your role. Or you can say you started reading a book called Job Spa that is helping strengthen your professional skills. "This is my first week in the book, so I'd like to make sure that I am meeting your expectations and that I understand any opportunities to improve" (or something to that effect).

We can hear you thinking, "What if my boss is vague and tells me I'm doing fine?" While it's better to hear that you are doing "fine" versus "not good," it does not necessarily help you to determine your strengths or opportunities for development. If you are unclear on what doing "fine" entails, probe a little bit more and ask what exactly she thinks is going well. What skills do you contribute to the group, and where can you utilize those skills on other projects down the road? In addition, ask if there is anything she recommends you do differently. Don't push it if she comes back with another vague answer. If you press too much, you may start to look insecure. Ask the question once, and see what you get.

Use the feedback your manager provides to confirm what you do well and identify opportunities for further development. In the future, ask for feedback regularly. At first, you may feel a little funny and a bit vulnerable asking someone to comment on how she or he thinks you are doing. After a few times, it will feel like a normal part of your job. Don't be a mushroom, live in darkness, and hope that what *you* think matches up with reality. Confirm your hopes by shining some light on your assumptions, and get yourself some well-deserved feedback. Record the highlights (strengths and areas for development) of what you hear. Keep these items on your radar screen as you work through your Job Spa.

Feedback from Your Teammates

Your teammates are a great source of information. Identify a few individuals with whom you are comfortable. Schedule a few minutes with them to review your feedback questions. Let them know you are working through this *Job Spa* book, and their feedback is really important to you.

Don't be surprised if the feedback you get back is more general than your manager's feedback. This may include, "You're doing great," or "Everyone seems to like you." Follow up with clarifying questions or get some examples. For instance, a follow up to "you're doing great" would be, "Is there something specific in what I'm doing that's great? I want to make sure to keep doing that." Similarly, a response to "I guess things are okay for the most part" would be, "What things could be better so that things are consistently okay or even great?"

If You Really Must Know . . .

The most important thing about asking for feedback from teammates is to ensure that there isn't some glaring behavior that you are missing that is annoying people to death. Although it might be a challenge to hear how your habit of scratching your head is making the team absolutely crazy (and it turns out that your nickname is "itchy"), it is more important to live in reality. Conclude by thanking the person for giving you feedback. Feedback can be tough to provide but imagine the sense of relief you'll feel when you know you're doing something well or know how to be more effective.

How to Ask

When requesting feedback, keep in mind these three rules:

1. *Ask about a specific event or behavior.* For example, "Bruce, how do you think I am doing regarding meeting our project deadlines? Are there any improvements or changes that I could make to be more effective?"
2. *Do not argue with the person giving feedback.* Instead, ask for specific examples of behaviors you displayed, others' reactions,

as well as recommendations for what you can do differently in the future. For example, "I really appreciate your feedback Bruce. I want to make sure that I understand the specific things that I can change. Will you give me an example of how I could have done a better job of setting expectations for completing my work?"

3. *Say thank-you.* Giving feedback is not easy for others. It can be perceived as risky for those who are concerned about upsetting you or sparking retaliation.

Since we're discussing the rules for asking for feedback, here are things to keep in mind if and when you are asked for feedback:

1. *Get permission:* Make sure you have permission to share. If you are taking the initiative to provide feedback without being prompted, asking permission is important to determine if this is a good time to share your observations. This puts the other person in control of the discussion and reduces defensiveness. For example, "I've been noticing something I want to share . . ." When there's an explicit agreement to provide feedback, you will increase the person's ability to listen and learn from your feedback.
2. *Make your motives clear:* Be clear about why you are giving feedback. Do not push your own agenda. Be explicit that you are giving feedback based on good intent. Adopt a caring attitude. Your language and words will follow. For example, "I'm sharing this because I think it will be helpful . . ."
3. *Be specific:* Describe the person's behavior, actions, and words precisely and accurately. Compare these comments: "Jane, you clearly don't like how I run our meetings. You don't make any suggestions at all. You are always distracted and not engaged." It's easy to see how this statement (while possibly true) would make Jane defensive and angry. Instead, be more specific: "Jane, I noticed in the meeting that you offered one comment and on a few occasions checked your e-mail. I'm wondering if everything's okay." This is a more accurate statement about someone's behavior. The statement in no way judges Jane but simply describes your

observations and asks her for her insights instead of drawing a conclusion about her intent.

4. *Be timely:* The closer the feedback occurs to the actual event, the easier it will be for people to remember what they did and adjust their behavior in the future.
5. *Regularity:* Establish a track record of providing feedback. This gives you more credibility when the going gets really tough and you have to deliver feedback that's not easy on the ears or ego.

Energy in Motion

Is it enough to just collect information from your manager and coworkers? Of course not! Getting the information is only the first step. It's time to review and act upon what you have learned.

As part of your commitment to your success, challenge yourself to take what you hear and set a goal of improving two to three things. Seriously consider any information you received regarding people's perception of your attitude toward work, the company, and the team. Demonstrate to the people around you that you are serious about your Job Spa success.

JOB SPA BONUS CHALLENGE

In addition to your manager, name two to three coworkers from whom you will ask for feedback.

Put It All Together

Wow! What an amazing first week with *Job Spa*. This was intensely rejuvenating and even a cleansing experience. You are off to a great start! You got clear on what it means to be committed to your success, and darn it, you are committed! Now it is time to put ideas into action. The best way to learn is by doing. Go through your week with your newfound attitude. See how your work world looks different through your new commitment lens. Reconnect with coworkers. This is your opportunity to practice your feedback skills. Get valuable information from coworkers about what you bring to the table and what you can do to be even more effective on the job.

Here is your calendar for the week. Plug in what you need to do to get rejuvenated and committed to your success!

Before you get ready for a well-deserved weekend, think back on this week. What went well? What did you learn? What do you want to work on or accomplish next week?

Congratulations on completing your first Job Spa week!

JOB SPA TREAT *for the* WEEK

Take yourself to lunch at your favorite spot.

Calendar for Week (1) Day (1) 2 3 4 5

Time	Action	Notes
6:00 A.M.		
7:00 A.M.		
8:00 A.M.		
9:00 A.M.		
10:00 A.M.		
11:00 A.M.		
12:00 P.M.		
1:00 P.M.		
2:00 P.M.		
3:00 P.M.		
4:00 P.M.		
5:00 P.M.		
6:00 P.M.		
7:00 P.M.		

REMINDERS

- Get clear on what you bring to the table. (Give 100 percent.)
- Get clear on what you need in return. (Take 100 percent.)
- Write down your commitment goals and reminders, and post them at home and work.
- Practice your feedback skills.
- Remove unnecessary distractions.
- Look for opportunities to contribute and help others.

Calendar for Week (1) Day 1 (2) 3 4 5

Time	*Action*	*Notes*
6:00 A.M.		
7:00 A.M.		
8:00 A.M.		
9:00 A.M.		
10:00 A.M.		
11:00 A.M.		
12:00 P.M.		
1:00 P.M.		
2:00 P.M.		
3:00 P.M.		
4:00 P.M.		
5:00 P.M.		
6:00 P.M.		
7:00 P.M.		

Calendar for Week (1) Day 1 2 (3) 4 5

Time	Action	Notes
6:00 A.M.		
7:00 A.M.		
8:00 A.M.		
9:00 A.M.		
10:00 A.M.		
11:00 A.M.		
12:00 P.M.		
1:00 P.M.		
2:00 P.M.		
3:00 P.M.		
4:00 P.M.		
5:00 P.M.		
6:00 P.M.		
7:00 P.M.		

Calendar for **Week (1) Day** 1 2 3 **(4)** 5

Time	*Action*	*Notes*
6:00 A.M.		
7:00 A.M.		
8:00 A.M.		
9:00 A.M.		
10:00 A.M.		
11:00 A.M.		
12:00 P.M.		
1:00 P.M.		
2:00 P.M.		
3:00 P.M.		
4:00 P.M.		
5:00 P.M.		
6:00 P.M.		
7:00 P.M.		

Calendar for Week (1) Day 1 2 3 4 (5)

Time	*Action*	*Notes*
6:00 A.M.		
7:00 A.M.		
8:00 A.M.		
9:00 A.M.		
10:00 A.M.		
11:00 A.M.		
12:00 P.M.		
1:00 P.M.		
2:00 P.M.		
3:00 P.M.		
4:00 P.M.		
5:00 P.M.		
6:00 P.M.		
7:00 P.M.		

week two
SET A NEW COURSE

"Last week I made some interesting realizations. I felt vulnerable asking for feedback, but it was worthwhile and a good reality check. I'm a little embarrassed that people noticed that I could be more engaged. It makes sense that if I am 100 percent committed to my success, I have to change my attitude about work and my contribution. It's really funny—all these years on the job and I never before asked what I want to give to my job and what I want in return. This is helping me focus on what is important to me. I am looking forward to setting my sights on new things and taking advantage of the opportunities that exist within my company.

"This Job Spa has also reminded me of the many coworkers whom I haven't spoken to in a while. When you're with a company for a while, you forget all the people you've come across. I guess it's never too late to reconnect.

"As I look around my company with this new perspective, I'm noticing things I haven't paid attention to in a while, like what 'success' looks like. Now that I've made my 100 Percent Commitment, I'll be paying more attention."

Welcome to Week Two!

Last week you identified what is important to you and made a commitment to your success. You stretched, toned, and took the first steps to workplace renewal. Your main objective this week is to set a course by identifying new opportunities and looking closer at *existing* opportunities. This week explore your surroundings with a fresh perspective.

The direction you set this week is up to you. You may decide on a plan to develop new skills and a path to a promotion. Or maybe you like your job and want to evaluate how you can try out new ideas. It's all up to you. Get what you need from your Job Spa. To help you make the most of your new objectives, establish a routine. Make sure your image and network supports your success. It's going to be a busy week, so pace yourself and stay focused. Your efforts in these early weeks will pay off!

WEEK 2	JOB SPA REGIMEN: SET A NEW DIRECTION
GOALS	Identify what you want to achieve.
TIME	Establish your routine.
KNOWLEDGE	Identify the opportunities.
TEAM	Assess your network.
IMAGE	Confirm the company image of success.

Goal

Last week you made a commitment to give and take as much as you can from your job: your 100 Percent Commitment. From the feedback you began to gather from your manager and coworkers, you realized how people at work perceive you. In what ways has this information affected how you now see yourself? What do you want as a result of being a part of your company? This week move your commitment forward. Take a fresh look at your current job, and stretch yourself to consider some new objectives that you can achieve, whether it is looking for opportunities in your current projects or creating new opportunities.

Take a Fresh Look

As part of establishing your Job Spa objectives, it is important that you take the initiative to re-examine your current role, responsibilities, and projects. Sometimes the best way to get to a new objective is to use your existing role or projects as a stepping stone. Additionally, now that you have an attitude that is focused and redirected to give and take 100 percent, you will see your work in a new light. Consider the following:

- What are the unrealized opportunities in my work and projects?
- What can I learn or gain from this experience?
- What projects, relationships, or other things around me can be turned into opportunities?
- What do I want to achieve over the next months and beyond?

One of the most important opportunities that you have as part of your Job Spa is to take a step back and re-evaluate your attitude, current role, responsibilities, and projects. With your new attitude, the things you took for granted as part of your job three weeks ago can become conduits to new possibilities.

From Aromatherapy to Hot Stone

It's easy to work day after day, changing course as obstacles or opportunities appear, and arrive months and even years down the road at a future that has either provided good fortune or perhaps a destiny that could have gone better. Your future should not be a random series of events but the result of setting a clear direction and achieving what you want. Sometimes this requires looking beyond your current role, responsibilities, and opportunities. What you want to achieve may include simply doing your existing job in a more effective manner or looking at new and bigger plans. If you want to consider more for yourself, ask yourself the following questions:

- What other kinds of projects do I want to be a part of?
- What new responsibilities would I like to have?
- What new skills or knowledge would I like to develop?
- What new relationships would I like to establish?
- What else do I want or need to accomplish?

For example, a Job Spa objective could be as big as creating a new and improved process for every client who buys your products through your company Web site. This will allow you to refine your current process, make it more efficient, increase the likelihood of additional purchases, allow you to use your creative skills, create relationships across the entire organization, and get visibility with key leaders. Ultimately, this objective ensures that you give your ideas and creativity to the company, you practice your team player skills, and you execute your plan. What you take in return is you lead a process improvement project (move aside Six Sigma Black Belts), you learn more and get trained in process improvement, you network, and you gain visibility.

Remember, a Job Spa objective can also be something less complex and more personal, such as focusing on producing higher quality work. This might entail thinking through ways in which you can be more thorough in your work, making the effort to explore various solutions and presenting a well-organized package. As a result, you feel a sense of achievement and your effort is recognized.

More than Words

Now let's take the ideas for your objectives and put them into a more concrete form. It's time to set some goals. In the User Instruction chapter, we introduced and outlined how to set effective goals. As you think about what you want, consider this: You increase the likelihood of both committing to and making your goal a reality if you stick to the basics of goal setting. Don't pooh-pooh this. It's amazing the number of people who can't set an effective goal whether they've been working for two years or twenty, whether they're an individual contributor or an executive.

The likelihood of accomplishing your goals is increased if you practice the following five steps:

1. *Commit to your goals:* Stay focused, and maintain momentum!
2. *Create achievable goals:* Set goals that are realistic, don't contradict one another, and are in your control.
3. *Determine what success looks like:* Imagine your finish line!
4. *Create a plan to get you to your goal:* Know where you are going and how you will get there!

Review the User Instruction chapter to refresh your goal-setting aptitude. Setting and achieving your goals is a very powerful tool for success. When you have clearly defined goals, you no longer sit back and wait for things to happen. Rather, you are an active participant and make things happen. You become your own champion. Clearly defined goals mean that every little thing you do is part of something bigger that you are building. It gives each task meaning and a bigger context. Having clear goals sets the stage for success.

Your goals can be either long-term (i.e., something achieved in one to five years and usually composed of specific and incremental short-term goals) or short-term (i.e., something that can be accomplished within a relatively short time, usually one week to six months). Examples of short-term goals include getting five new clients in the next four months or leaving work on time to make your kid's swim meets this season.

As part of your Job Spa, identify one special thing that you want to achieve over the next eleven weeks. This goal may be in conjunction with other Job Spa goals or completely unique. Make this something that you can claim as an accomplishment by the time you finish this book. Take a second to think about this. Okay, let's continue.

Bond with Your Goal

After you identify your goals, you will need to answer one important question: Why do you want this? Let's say one of your goals is to initiate and lead a new project. What about this goal motivates you? You may decide that initiating and leading a new project will take your experience to the next level, will be good for your resume, and give you a sense of accomplishment. Clearly understanding why you want something provides you with two very important things: momentum while you work toward your objective, and gratification once you reach your goal.

Get clear on why you want something. For instance, when someone asks for a promotion, what is it that he is really asking for? If you dig deeper and ask what the promotion will do for him, you find out that what he really wants is recognition and a bigger salary but not necessarily more responsibility. You realize that there are alternatives to satisfying his underlying interests.

Similarly, as you look at your goal, ask "If I get ___________, what will that do for me? Is that what I really want?" This will help you identify the right goal and at times show you the easiest path to your destination. You will feel more gratification when you reach your goal.

Create Achievable Goals

Why in the world would someone create a goal that's not achievable? Many goals start off with great intentions but are either too broad or vague to be achieved. For example, here is a goal that you have probably heard and perhaps considered: *I'm going to become CEO because I can do a better job.* Hats off to you! Is it realistic? It can be. However, identifying the goal of becoming CEO is huge! Consider a more attainable goal that will lead to your larger goal. While keeping the bigger goal of becoming CEO on your radar screen, look at the steps it will take to achieve. Do you need an MBA? Do you need to hone your leadership skills? Can you stomach an eighty-hour work week and the pressure of Sarbanes-Oxley?

Set a goal you can achieve and that's right for you. Stretch yourself, of course, but make sure it's realistic and thought out. Here are some ways you can ensure your goal is achievable:

- *Alignment:* Your goal is consistent with your work environment, values, personal objectives, and where you want to be in the future.
- *Control:* You have influence over what you want to achieve.
- *Trajectory:* You can define the steps to get from here to there.

Success Factors

Imagine running a race with no finish line. That's what you are doing when you have not explicitly identified what you want to achieve as a result of accomplishing a goal. How will you know that you've reached your goal? You will know that you've crossed your finish line when you've identified up-front, specific, clear markers. As you think about what you want to achieve, determine the success factors:

- *See:* What will you see that indicates you've achieved your goal?
- *Hear:* What will you be saying to other people or hear others say that lets you know you've achieved your goal?
- *Feel:* How will you feel when you've achieved your goal?

Use this week to think through your Job Spa objectives. Next week, you will put a plan into place.

JOB SPA BONUS CHALLENGE

Identify your one special Job Spa goal that you want to achieve over the next eleven weeks.

Time

Now that you have revisited your world with a fresh perspective and identified your trajectory, ensure that your goals have every chance of success. This brings us to the all-important skill of time management. Time is a key component to ensuring that your goals become a reality.

Make Your Routine Work

As part of your Job Spa, balance your inner time-management chi. The first step, grasshopper, is to start off with the basics of time management: a routine. As mundane as this might sound, defining a routine is one of the first steps in turning time management from a concept into a skill. The idea of a routine might sound confining and boring. Stay with us. Some things in life *are* boring, especially when it comes to establishing predictability and a flow for how and when you get things done. An effective routine sets you up for success and minimizes surprises.

Having a routine means bringing predictability into your work life. In turn, predictability allows you to be flexible. You can quickly make changes because you readily know what your schedule can accommodate. Establish a routine that is consistent and predictable so you can manage your schedule, work, and minimize stress.

Snooze, You Lose

A great way to start understanding and using a routine is to create a morning routine. The start of your day sets the stage for how you will approach the rest of the day. Many people do not give themselves enough time and end up running out of the house with two different colored socks, no coffee, and a pissed-off five-year-old with a sack lunch that's missing her favorite cookie. When you have a routine, you know how many times you can hit the snooze button and still get to work on time—unstressed and ready to go.

Note: the best strategy to developing an effective morning routine is to work backward. Begin by identifying when you are expected at work. If your company starts at 8:30 A.M., calculate the following:

- How long it takes to get from your car to your cube/office and log on to your computer
- How long it takes to get from home to work, accounting for traffic
- How long it takes to eat breakfast
- How long it takes to take care of things like kids, pets, and spouses
- How long it takes to get from bed to being dressed

What time do you need to go to bed in order to get a full night's sleep?

Before you know it, what you thought was a half-hour routine to get out of the house and on your way to work is really an hour, and you find yourself pulling up to the company parking lot at 8:55. What happened? Life happened. Starting your day rushed and behind will leave a negative residue on the rest of your day. Give yourself plenty of time. Make sure you account for distractions and interruptions.

It's time to make adjustments to those ingrained behaviors. Get up ten minutes earlier if need be. Give yourself the opportunity to start off on the right foot to ensure your success. "But those extra ten minutes of sleep are so precious in the morning," you argue. Yes, they certainly are. What's more important to you? An extra ten minutes of sleep or fulfilling your 100 Percent Commitment to your success? You make the choice.

Happy Hour . . . Not So Fast

No day would be complete without a routine for bringing your day to a close. Are you leaving at a decent hour? Do you find yourself pushing things out to the last hour of your day? A well-thought-through end-of-day routine will help you wrap up loose ends from the current day and let you prepare for the next day. If your goal is to be home by 6:30 P.M., but you keep getting home at 7:00, did you account for certain things?

- The five minutes to log off your computer system
- Ten minutes talking to Emily on your way out about the strange meeting earlier that day
- Five minutes to get to your car
- Ten minutes to pick up dry cleaning

Establishing a routine for bringing your day to a close will help you create a smooth transition between your work day and your evening. Think through the steps that will help you close out the current day, prepare for tomorrow, and transition to life after work. Thinking through various routines will help you become more cognizant of time and your pace, and help you respond to issues more effectively.

Head in the Clouds or Feet on the Ground?

Between your morning and when it's time to pack it up and head home is that block of time you spend going to meetings, sending e-mails, and "working." Job Spa success requires that you make the most of your time. In addition to your routine, it is critical that you align your internal clock with the external clock.

Your internal clock or how you experience time (i.e., time in *your* mind) may not be correlated with the external clock on your wall or desk. The higher the degree of alignment between your internal clock and the external clock, the easier it will be to accurately plan and track your activities.

For instance, when you are talking with someone you meet in the hallway, do you realize during your conversation that ten minutes have passed, or did it feel like a minute? If your internal clock is out of alignment, interruptions will take up more time than you realize.

Your ability to keep track of the passage of time is a key to your ability to manage your time effectively. Get in the habit of keeping track of time and how much time it takes to complete various activities. Your objective is to become more cognizant of time, to recognize how you spend time, and to ensure that you allow enough time to accomplish all your tasks in such a way that you are not stressed. Your awareness of how long it takes to get things done will put you in a better position to accurately forecast and communicate project status and ultimately support your Job Spa goal. Use this week to make your routines work for you. Next week, you'll build upon your time-management skills and create a realistic time line and plan for your Job Spa goal.

JOB SPA BONUS CHALLENGE

Refine your morning or evening routine.

Knowledge

In Week Two you have taken a closer look at the opportunities and possibilities that surround you. Before declaring complete and total workplace enlightenment, take a peek around to ensure that you are setting the right objectives and have the information you need to make the right decisions.

School Your Inner Child

In a constantly changing world, it is important to stay ahead of the curve by learning and adapting. The key to staying one step ahead is to understand how to identify developing trends in your profession, company, industry, and the broader economy. This will allow you to effectively set goals that are relevant today and tomorrow. With respect to your Job Spa goal, information about upcoming trends will inform the relevancy and impact of your goal to both you and your company.

Examples of trends include economic trends such as the move from regional to global markets, sales trends such as the increase in your company's sales over the course of three quarters, consumer patterns such as the move from SUVs to smaller hybrid cars, or breakthrough products that can influence or create an entire industry such as the advent of the personal computer. As you think through your 100 Percent Commitment, look at how to get more engaged with your current and future projects. What trends do you need to take into consideration?

- *At a team level,* what teaming and collaboration trends have you noticed? Is it more important and valued to start a project by first collaborating with others or by running off and doing it alone?
- *At a company level,* what project trends get more visibility? How does this impact the kind of projects you want to work on? How does this impact your desired career path at your company?
- *At an industry level,* what kinds of products and services get recognized? What trends have you noticed around consumer/client behaviors? How does this impact your goals?
- *At an economic level,* where are the largest pockets for economic growth and sustainability? How does this impact any of your goals? Does a larger, sustainable force support your project and career goals?

Take these factors into consideration as you review current projects and look for opportunities to increase what you can strategically contribute. By reviewing these strategic elements, you might come up with a creative or new angle in which to approach your projects, make your contribution, and collaborate with coworkers.

JOB SPA BONUS CHALLENGE

Identify two new sources of business or industry information.

Team

A big part of making the most of your work environment is continually building and reinforcing the network of relationships you have with coworkers and professionals outside of your job. Your network should be a dependable, ever-evolving resource. As part of setting your new objectives, determine where you need to expand your network or reinforce existing relationships to be more effective and get what you need.

Tone and Stretch Your Relationships

Do you consider yourself to be buried treasure waiting for discovery by your ignorant teammates? Think it's their responsibility to figure out what an amazing source of skills, knowledge, and potential you are? Think again. It's your job to make sure that they are aware of what you have to offer. Luckily, it's never too late to get out there. Announce to the world what you have to share, and build your network.

Your network is the culmination of relationships and connections that you have available through the people you know. Building and expanding your network can be as easy as introducing yourself to people as you pass them in the halls. Say, "I've been here for three years now, and I don't think we've been introduced. I'm Harry . . . " You can also identify people you want to meet and schedule introductory meetings with them. No matter how long you've been with the company, you always need to grow your network.

Okay, so you feel silly for not having reached out before, or perhaps, small talk is just not your thing. To make it even easier, here are some additional discussion topics for when you meet old coworkers for the first time. Ask about:

- History and experience in the company
- Current role and corresponding responsibilities
- Insights or knowledge that pertains to your work
- Who else they think you should meet

As you engage in light banter, listen for opportunities to volunteer your resources, connections, or information. Making this early effort to contribute will do wonders to build trust. Most important, others will be compelled to give up the goods when you ask the classic Networking 101 question: "Is there anyone else that you think I should talk with about _________."

Assess Your Network

Maybe you're feeling as if you can skip this section. You've been at the same job long enough to know everyone around you. You're feeling cozy. You know enough people that if you needed information on anything, you could get it in minutes, right? We challenge you to a friendly review. Assess your network to determine how it can grow. A healthy network is a web of relationships composed of three levels:

1. The first level of your network is made up of your relationships with family, friends and colleagues. These are people with whom you have direct contact. This may include a range of relationships from the people you socialize with on a regular basis to colleagues you have lunch with once or twice a year. Picture this as your inner circle of contacts and the core of your network.

2. The second level of your network is made up of people who are friends of friends. You don't have a direct relationship with these people. For example, you are at a dinner party, and one of your friends mentions that she is having dinner with a friend next week who is the CEO of a *Fortune* 500 company. How exciting, you think . . . you know someone who knows someone who's a CEO. You've now got a connection into a *Fortune* 500! Picture this second level as the middle ring of your network.
3. The third level of your network is composed of people with whom you do not have a relationship at all; you know them only through indirect relationships. For instance, your friend's CEO buddy knows your favorite chef. How exciting! However, this in no way impacts your ability to get reservations at the hottest restaurant in town.

Levels 1 and 2 are extremely important to networking. How do you know your network is sufficient? Do you have access to a broad network of people who possess knowledge, resources, and also know a range of people? If you only hang out with two coworkers and have met only five other people in your organization of 250, you need to push yourself to meet more people. If your pool of potential network people is limited, develop relationships with those who *do* have strong networks so you can piggyback off their network (i.e., rely on Level 2).

Think about your 100 Percent Commitment, look at your network of colleagues and create a list based on the following questions:

- Who are the people who compose my network?
- What other people can I / should I meet using my existing connections (Level 1), so I create more relationships and possibilities?
- What additional people do I need to meet, so I have access to a greater depth and wealth of knowledge?
- How can I leverage all three levels of my network to get there?

Your network is one of the key components to helping you gain momentum toward your success and sustain that success over time. In addition, one of the top reasons people are motivated to stay in their current position is that they like their coworkers and have established a network that supports them professionally. It makes work a more enjoyable place. Thinking ahead, when the time comes to change jobs, your network will be there to provide leads, connections, and support.

JOB SPA BONUS CHALLENGE

Create a list of people in the first and second levels of your network.

Image

Close your eyes and picture someone successful. This person probably has a culmination of traits: appearance, communication, and behaviors that create your perception. Close your eyes again and now picture yourself. Are you your ideal vision of success? There are many factors that contribute to professional success. Quality work and productivity are important, but they will only get you so far.

Presenting yourself in a manner that is intentional and consistent with how you want to be known is a must. You want to be the total package: the looks, behaviors, and results. Confirm that you are on course. Take a look around to see how coworkers who are considered effective or successful dress, communicate, and do their jobs. Identify what your company and coworkers view as successful. Confirm the specific behaviors that get recognized and rewarded. Let's go back to the Image Salon and take a closer look. What can you do to reinforce your image to help you achieve your Job Spa goal?

A Holistic Perspective

Last week you took the feedback challenge by gathering feedback from your manager and trusted coworkers. This week continue to identify opportunities for a little Job Spa makeover. Think you are dressing for success with a look that says "winner"? Little do you know that your coworkers in finance, who never wear jeans, call you Mr. Casual when you're not around. You might be working hard and doing a good job, but if you aren't stopping to look around, you may be in for a surprise.

Here are questions that can help you with image alignment:

- How are the leaders in my company dressed?
- How are my coworkers dressed?
- How do I compare?

You may want to fit in with your coworkers, but if your goal is to be a leader in the company, kick it up a notch while still fitting in. Use sound judgment. Keep the Hawaiian shirts for the company barbecue. Pay attention to all of these subtle elements. When effectively applied, each detail adds up to an image of strength and success.

Odds are you probably know what it takes to be successful in your company. You've probably always known. You also have limits about what you are willing to do to ensure your success. As part of your Job Spa, re-evaluate what you want or need to adjust to ensure that you are giving and taking 100 percent. It is possible that part of giving 100 percent requires making an effort to enhance your image. This may include dressing, communicating, and behaving differently. Furthermore, as you think about how you can enhance your current projects or create new opportunities, how will a stronger professional image support you? What would that look like?

It's your call if you decide that you are not going to give up wearing T-shirts, even though all your peers wear button-down shirts. Be forewarned, if you are doing it on principle alone (because you don't want to give up your identity as the rebel), you are not 100 percent committed to your success. You are purposely sabotaging yourself.

There are some things worth giving up and other things worth holding onto. Make strategic choices that support your success.

Define That Certain Something

Besides dress, what are the characteristics of effective leaders in the company? Is it a look, a style of communicating, or the ability to make others comfortable? What do these individuals appear to know, what skills do they have, and what behaviors do they exhibit? You may find that the truly effective people are not the ones who know everything and can regurgitate facts, figures, and business models at the slightest provocation. Instead, they are able to apply what they know, see the big picture, communicate their ideas, and inspire others. Which traits do you notice that you would like to add to your repertoire?

What Gets Heard

Of all the things that you hear each day, what are the characteristics of what you hear that actually stick? What words, expressions, or tone of voice stays in your mind? Try the following: Think about all of your interactions yesterday. What conversations stand out? What topics, statements, or words resonate? Consider how much of what you say actually gets cemented in other people's minds? As you continue observing the people around you, pay attention to what causes people to perk up.

A good place to begin zeroing in on effective communication techniques is to observe how successful people communicate. What makes them effective? Are they polite and ask lots of good questions? Do they support what they say with facts or references? When you walk away after a conversation with them, what strikes you as important to them? Effective communicators have a clear message, speak at the appropriate level of detail, and ask questions that promote further exchange of ideas. Combined, these characteristics reinforce their message and ensure that what they say is remembered. What can you do to refine your communication style to help achieve your Job Spa goal?

JOB SPA BONUS CHALLENGE

Identify three successful people who have qualities you would like to emulate.

Put It All Together

Congratulations on your second week of Job Spa. You've spent this week dipping into what you want by leveraging existing opportunities and defining new ones. You've removed the cucumber slices from your eyes to reveal a whole new perspective on how people communicate and behave. Support your 100 Percent Commitment by building your network and reinforcing your image. Get your morning, daytime, and evening routine dialed in.

It's also time to put your observations and ideas into action. Here is your calendar for the week. Plug in what you need to do in Week Two to get rejuvenated and committed to your success! Before you get ready for a well-deserved weekend, think back on the week. What went well? What did you learn? What do you want to work on or accomplish next week?

Congratulations on completing your second Job Spa week!

JOB SPA TREAT for the WEEK

Infuse your office/cube with a little life. Bring in fresh flowers, an orchid, or even a bonsai tree.

Calendar for Week (2) Day (1) 2 3 4 5

Time	*Action*	*Notes*
6:00 A.M.		
7:00 A.M.		
8:00 A.M.		
9:00 A.M.		
10:00 A.M.		
11:00 A.M.		
12:00 P.M.		
1:00 P.M.		
2:00 P.M.		
3:00 P.M.		
4:00 P.M.		
5:00 P.M.		
6:00 P.M.		
7:00 P.M.		

REMINDERS

- As part of your Job Spa objective, look for opportunities to leverage your current projects and make them better.
- Reconnect with coworkers by asking them to lunch and setting up meetings.
- Get clear on the image of success in your company and what you are willing to do differently to ensure your success.
- Get your morning, daytime, and evening routine under control.

Calendar for **Week (2) Day** 1 (2) 3 4 5

Time	*Action*	*Notes*
6:00 A.M.		
7:00 A.M.		
8:00 A.M.		
9:00 A.M.		
10:00 A.M.		
11:00 A.M.		
12:00 P.M.		
1:00 P.M.		
2:00 P.M.		
3:00 P.M.		
4:00 P.M.		
5:00 P.M.		
6:00 P.M.		
7:00 P.M.		

Calendar for Week (2) Day 1 2 (3) 4 5

Time	Action	Notes
6:00 A.M.		
7:00 A.M.		
8:00 A.M.		
9:00 A.M.		
10:00 A.M.		
11:00 A.M.		
12:00 P.M.		
1:00 P.M.		
2:00 P.M.		
3:00 P.M.		
4:00 P.M.		
5:00 P.M.		
6:00 P.M.		
7:00 P.M.		

Calendar for Week (2) Day 1 2 3 (4) 5

Time	Action	Notes
6:00 A.M.		
7:00 A.M.		
8:00 A.M.		
9:00 A.M.		
10:00 A.M.		
11:00 A.M.		
12:00 P.M.		
1:00 P.M.		
2:00 P.M.		
3:00 P.M.		
4:00 P.M.		
5:00 P.M.		
6:00 P.M.		
7:00 P.M.		

Calendar for Week (2) Day 1 2 3 4 (5)

Time	Action	Notes
6:00 A.M.		
7:00 A.M.		
8:00 A.M.		
9:00 A.M.		
10:00 A.M.		
11:00 A.M.		
12:00 P.M.		
1:00 P.M.		
2:00 P.M.		
3:00 P.M.		
4:00 P.M.		
5:00 P.M.		
6:00 P.M.		
7:00 P.M.		

week three
CREATE A PLAN

"Here I am in Week Three of what I'm now calling my Job Spa treatment. I looked around last week at my environment and got reconnected with coworkers. In these conversations and reflections, I realized there are opportunities for me to take advantage of what are already part of my existing projects and role. There are also clearly other new opportunities that I'm excited about. All of a sudden it seems like there are many opportunities, and I want to make sure that I don't throw too much stuff on my plate. I've decided to set some initial goals that are doable and excite me.

"I'm laughing at myself because I know my manager offered to pay for some training programs nine months ago, and I didn't really bother to think about what new skills I wanted that will help my professional development. Now that I have a destination in mind, I just need to put a plan into place to get me there."

Welcome to Week Three!

Last week you zeroed in on what you want to achieve and cranked up your energy. You looked at your current work, projects, and responsibilities with a perspective that was as fresh as a mint-and-seaweed facial scrub. You also took a deep breath and meditated on what new objectives you want to bring into reality.

This week you will transform your big ideas into a plan that includes identifying the resources needed to achieve your goals. To ensure that you are becoming a nimble cubicle ninja, hone your image skills by developing your listening proficiency. Keep your calendar up-to-date and equipped to support your plans.

WEEK 3	JOB SPA REGIMEN: GET READY
GOALS	Create a plan.
TIME	Manage your calendar (based on the new plan).
KNOWLEDGE	Identify what you know, what you need to know, and additional required resources.
TEAM	Identify existing and new coworkers you need to meet.
IMAGE	Practice active listening skills.

Goal

Last week you thought through what you want to achieve as part of your 100 Percent Commitment. Now that you have a better idea of your destination, it's time to figure out how to get there. Like a climber in the Himalayas, you need a Sherpa to see you through. In less dramatic terms you need a plan as you navigate the sea of cubicles, Francine in Finance, and a host of office obstacles to see you safely to your Nirvana. Unlike other unwary predecessors who have laughed at fate and scoffed at the idea of a plan, you know better. Your plan will confirm your destination, identify the critical steps that will get you there, and discover the resources you will need.

Plan Your Goal

You have a goal in mind; now let's chart a course to get you from where you are to your future. Defining what you want is not as simple as saying, "I want to be part of a project that will lead to a promotion in six months." The first step to wrangle your goals into a tidy plan is to break them into smaller pieces. Grab a piece of paper or start up your computer, it's time to identify:

1. *Goal(s):* What you want to achieve (from last week).
2. *Resources:* What you need to get the job done. Resource planning will help you reach your goal.
3. *Milestones:* Defining the major milestones allows you to better manage your progress and maintain direction.
4. *Timeline:* Document your milestones in your calendar. Make your deadlines realistic, and hold yourself to them.
5. *Task List:* Create and use a task list of the action items required on a weekly basis to get to your milestones. This ensures that you stay on track to reach your goal and enables you to look back on what you accomplished.

As you raise your head and look at the future, it is critical that you first take care of the business at hand. If possible, align your new Job Spa goals with your current work. It will be easier to manage your workload and time. If this is not possible, it is important to balance the demands of your job with the demands of achieving additional Job Spa objectives.

Every Step You Take

Remember that cross-country road trip when you where a kid to Aunt Bessie's? You made a bunch of stops along the way: the giant cheese ball, the worlds largest scab collection, and that odd museum of prosthetic devices. You also probably made some unintended stops, like when little Ernie couldn't wait to stop to share the side effects of the all-you-can-eat taco night. Similar to the various stops on your road trip, an effective plan contains key steps or milestones that you need to attain along the path to achieving your goal.

Define your milestones so you will have a clear trajectory and definitive understanding of where you are going and what you will need. Milestones will help you prioritize, bridging the chasm between you and your lovely goals with a series of tangible steps. If you are not already familiar with breaking your goals down into milestones, practice it with your existing projects. Take a look at your work and the key steps that are involved in its completion. Next, review your Job Spa goals. Identify the significant milestones.

As a preview into next week, be prepared to share your plan containing milestones with your manager. This will demonstrate that you are taking your current projects seriously and thinking about how to make your projects even better. It also helps to get her input so that she feels part of the process and is emotionally invested in your success. Note: Next week we'll talk about how to deal with your manager if your goals are beyond your current work, and you think your manager is threatened by your newfound motivation.

Cash, Check, or Corporate Karma

Having the necessary resources is *very* important.You don't want to get worked up and ready to conquer the world only to realize that you are not prepared to go the distance.As Uncle Seever used to say, you don't bring a football to a basketball game.Well, so much for family words of wisdom. In other words, know where you're going and what you'll need to get you there.

Carefully think through what you need before you launch toward your goal. Clearly define the resources you need, where and how to get them, when you will need them, and what you can and can't live without. Define your resource inventory.Your predefined inventory will ensure that you prepared for success and maintain momentum. Resources can include dollars, time, people, skills, and fuzzy pink bunnies (are you paying attention?).

Be realistic, flexible, and a bit creative to ensure you have the resources you require. The quest for resources might be hampered by limited company budgets, opportunities, or time. As you know from experience, resources can be scarce. Have a backup plan in case you don't get what you need. Be ready to negotiate if necessary. Don't have your goal stopped at the launch pad.

Once you have identified the resources, it's time to go get them. As you know, sometimes that process may take a while. You may need to ask your manager and other colleagues for their time. Ensure that your plan takes these potential delays into account.

Scarcity is a fact of organizational life. When it comes time to ask for the handout, be prepared with a clear concise case for your request. If you don't get what you requested, change gears, skip to Plan B, and look for opportunities to negotiate alternatives. Remember to stay professional, be resourceful, and maintain a can-do attitude.

JOB SPA BONUS CHALLENGE

Have your plan, timeline, and correlating resources ready to review with your manager before next week.

Time

As you limber up and prepare to sprint to your destiny, make sure that you allocate and manage your time in conjunction with your goals. Now that your plan is taking shape, this is a good time to add relevant dates and deadlines. Do you have Job Spa goals that are beyond your current role? Even if it's only fifteen minutes every other day, allocate time in your calendar to work on your goals. Stay on top of your task list by identifying the specifics of what you need to do on a day-to-day basis. Use these time-management tools to help you maintain focus and discipline.

"But I already know this," you respond. Well, if we didn't put it in here, you'd accuse us of forgetting about something so basic! Let's go.

Deadline Dates

As you know from experience, no healthy plan would be complete without locking down specific dates. Begin by adding a date for reaching your goal. Then work backward, adding dates for each milestone. Consider the resources you need and if there are any timing issues because of availability. Are your dates realistic, given current demands?

Ponder the influence of your work habits as you exercise your date-setting prowess. If you have a tendency to wait until the last minute to get things done, consider giving yourself early deadlines and front-load the bulk of the tasks. If your goals will take a number of months to accomplish, try putting the majority of the milestones and tasks in the first few months of your plan. This way you will feel more pressure to start immediately and not procrastinate. If procrastination is not a threat, a more evenly laid-out plan might suit your needs. Know thyself and plan accordingly.

As you work backward from the end of your goal, consider if you have given yourself enough or even too much time. As eager as you are to show how quickly you can get something done, give yourself enough time, and account for the unexpected. We all know it's always better to deliver something early or on time than late. As part of demonstrating your 100 Percent Commitment, make every effort to follow through and successfully reach your deadlines.

Use Your Calendar

Your calendar is not there to look pretty. It is for daily consumption. Is this too basic for you? We're delighted to get that response. On a scale of one to ten, are you a perfect ten? Probably not. Here are reminders to help keep you in line. Revisit it at least twice a day:

- *In the morning when you start your day*—this will get you focused.
- *At the end of the day*—this will prepare you for the next day.

Fill your calendar with meetings, events, milestones, reminders, and deadlines. Here are three additional rules of thumb to follow to effectively manage your time.

1. Immediately update your calendar as events and deadlines shift.
2. Do not double-book your meetings. You may think this shows you're an important person, but the impression you leave is that you are disorganized or not respectful of other people's time. The same goes for talking to other people and writing e-mails while talking on the phone. It's rude (and yes, people can hear the click of the keys on the other end of the phone).
3. Back-to-back-to-back appointments do not set you up for time-management success unless you are very good at cutting off a conversation as you dash to another meeting. These marathon meetings are intense, and you are expected to be "on" for hours in a row. The likelihood is that you will be running from one meeting to the next in a hopeless state of tardiness. There are times back-to-back meetings cannot be avoided. If so, you can let others know that it's important that you make your next meeting on time. "But will I look like a jerk who thinks the world revolves around me?" No need to worry. If you are explicit that it is important to *you* that you are on time for *all* of your meetings, people will understand.

For those of you familiar with these problems, identify one thing you can do consistently to take you to time-management mastery.

Task Lists

It's time to bask in the glory of minutia: task lists help take things down to a level of specificity you've always wanted but may not have taken the time to do. This is your opportunity to clean house and create a task list as you re-examine your current work load and look at new goals.

Here are the two steps to help you get there.

1. *General task list:* Create and maintain a general task list of the major projects/items in which you are involved, including your 100 Percent Commitment goals. This list helps you see the big picture at all times.
2. *Daily task list:* From the general task list, create a daily task list of both current project tasks and new Job Spa–related tasks. This list contains items you need to accomplish on a daily basis to keep you focused and organized.

Beyond projects, your task list is a great way to stay on top of all the little things that need to get done: that document for your coworker, those follow-up calls, and the review of that document your teammate requested. Your task list will help you knock out all those little extra tasks, ensure that nothing falls between the cracks, and help you continually embody your 100 Percent Commitment.

As you go through your Job Spa, use the time-management tools we've discussed. These tools are critical to help you stay on track and prepare for the uncharted waters ahead. As you know, effective time management is not rocket science; it just takes a bit of discipline and a desire to make the most of your time.

Prioritize, Prioritize, and Prioritize!

Your mighty goal is only as good as your ability to plan *and* deliver. As part of giving and taking 100 percent, it is critical that you follow through. You don't want to be the guy who likes to talk about his great new ideas and plans but never shows results. In the day-to-day bustle of getting your work done, it's so easy to be distracted and lose focus on your plans. You must actively manage yourself and consistently understand where to allocate your time.

Perhaps, your Job Spa goals can be achieved as part of your current job and projects. Or your goals may require additional training or work outside your daily activities. When do you have time for that? There is so much to do! Keep focused, and maintain momentum toward accomplishing your goals by prioritizing your work. You will be amazed at your ability to squeeze out the time you need to get it all done.

You will need to balance your time a bit if new objectives are outside your immediate role and responsibilities. In the excitement of mapping out your new plans to reframe your current project or look for new opportunities, don't forget that your current projects are still your top priority. Your manager is expecting results and you need to deliver on your current work. Part of a successful Job Spa is learning to balance the demands of today with charting your path to tomorrow. Maintaining this duality requires you to prioritize immediate deliverables while managing to keep an eye on the future.

JOB SPA BONUS CHALLENGE

Create a daily task list right now.

Knowledge

As you work through your plans this week, you may begin to realize you are getting a bit dehydrated and thirsty. You thirst not for a cooling sports drink but for yummy, replenishing, yet surprisingly low-calorie knowledge. As you work through your plans, satiate your thirst for knowledge this week by focusing on what valuable information you will need.

Reinventing the Wheel

For thousands of years humans have had the ability to document and share information: from cave paintings to printing presses to blogging. No matter what the medium, it's painful to consider how often the same work of discovery is done again and again. To maximize your time, resources, and effectiveness, determine what resources or knowledge currently exists so you don't reinvent the wheel to get to your Job Spa goal. Start with the resources that are available around you. Teammates and coworkers are a good source of information. Do a thorough job of identifying the people and information that impact your projects.

No matter what you are working on, odds are that others somewhere have walked a similar path. It saves you and your company time, money, and effort when you identify and build upon existing work. This can even inspire new ideas and better ways of solving a problem.

Don't be too proud to ask for help. There are tons of lessons and great bits of knowledge to be gathered from coworkers and teammates. Get insight on the subtleties and wisdom they have on a topic, their success, or any obstacles they have encountered. Leave no stone or coworker unturned. Okay, so don't turn over your coworkers. Ask them about what you are looking for. You may be very surprised to realize that the guy you have had lunch with for the past two years is an expert in a wide range of fields.

As you conclude each of your conversations, always ask, "Is there anybody else you think I should talk to about this?" No matter how dry a well of knowledge your current contact might be, they may have connections that will provide the information you seek (and build your Level 1 network).

WE'RE NOT ASKING you to plagiarize. Obey all patent, trademarks, and copyright laws. In addition, give your contributors their due. Publicly thank people for their knowledge and give them credit. This is extremely important unless you want to quickly torch your bridges. You want to build trust and a foundation for further collaboration.

Develop Your Own Skills

Need to present your project plan in a few weeks but have rusty presentation skills? Think a degree in marketing would be great for helping develop new product strategies for your company's products? Although you may have the biggest brain from your family's gene pool, you may start to find that there are areas in which it would be helpful to acquire additional knowledge and skills.

Your immediate priority is to define the short-term development you need as part of your current projects and to reach your Job Spa goals. Identify what programs are available (internal and/or external to the company) and ensure they are timely, so you can get the skills and information you need as quickly as possible. Make changes to existing project plans based on any training you might need.

For longer-term skill development, start a running list of the skills and knowledge you want to acquire. Refer to this list when opportunities to discuss your skill development interests come up with your manager. Remember, when you continually develop your skills, you make yourself more marketable and valuable.

JOB SPA BONUS CHALLENGE

This week, identify and share something of value with your team or coworkers.

Team

As you continue down the planning path, take an even closer look at your network. No matter if you have been at your company for one year or twenty years, it is imperative that you continue to build and reinforce your relationships. A well-tuned network means that you can pick up the phone or send an e-mail to one of your colleagues. The answer to an important question or resource will be on its way. Let's assess your current network to determine if it's on life support, in need of a shot of adrenaline, or healthy and only needs some vitamins.

What Do Your Friends Know, Anyway?

Think about the different areas of expertise each of the individuals in your network has. Who has what information? For example, in your network you may find that Burt has strong research skills. He can get you any kind of information you need, from the latest government product regulations in France to what your department vice president likes to have for lunch. Mary knows everyone in finance and can get your purchase order processed quickly. Emma knows the bigwigs in academia and is always on top of the latest economic forecasts for your company's industry. With associates like these, who needs the CIA?

Do you have the network you need? What other kind of knowledge would be helpful? Finally, who do you need to meet? Do you have the right people with the right information as part of your network to help you reach your Job Spa goals?

Here are the four steps you can take to determine how to leverage your network (reference your work last week with your network levels 1 and 2):

1. What information or knowledge is required to do your job and reach your Job Spa goals? What information do you have and what kind of information requires you to tap into your network? What kind of information do you need as part of your new Job Spa objectives?
2. Who do you know, and what do they know? Review your list from last week. Have these colleagues been helpful to you when you needed something? Are they the right people with the right information?
3. Who else has additional information, knowledge, or access that would be helpful? Do your colleagues know anyone who may be helpful?
4. In return for what they can give, what information or other resources do you have that would be of value to them?

This assessment is an important exercise. It gives you a realistic picture of what you can expect from your current network and helps you consider what additional relationships are required to achieve your goals.

More than just lunch buddies, your network is there to serve a purpose. So don't feel shy about assessing who you know and who else would be helpful to get to know. It doesn't mean you dump your old coworkers for new ones. Like adding more time to your massage, you can't go wrong by adding more folks to your network.

Reaching Out

Perhaps in the past you have not been a very social person. Besides, that cubicle of yours is just so cozy. Yes, sometimes it is easier not to make the effort and reach out to people. Things have changed; you are now 100 percent committed to your success. Who do you need to meet, and how do you go about meeting them?

Start a conversation, get an introduction, and perhaps initiate a meeting. If you have a list of people you need to meet, great. Send them an e-mail inviting them to a meeting or to lunch. In your introduction, indicate why you would like to meet them. For example, "Hi, Emma, I understand you are on top of the latest in economic forecasts. Would you like to have lunch? I'd like to find out more of your thoughts on the predictions for next year as I'm putting together a proposal for a new project." If you do not have a targeted list, go to your manager and coworkers and ask them who else you should meet.

JOB SPA BONUS CHALLENGE

Meet two new work-related people this week.

Image

As discussed in the Team section, a big part of making the most of your Job Spa is to continuously meet people and build your network. These interactions also provide a great opportunity to brush up on your communication skills. It's time to look closer at the underutilized and bigger piece of the conversational duo of talking and listening.

Active Listening

Although this is *your* Job Spa, make ample space in the Sauna, Steam Room, and Mineral Bath for others. In line with this sharing philosophy, it is important to demonstrate in your conversations that you are listening to the other person. While active listening is one of those overused terms in the soft-skill set, it is nevertheless an extremely important skill that even the bigwigs are not really good at. So get a leg up on the competition and hone your active-listening skills. The basics of active listening include:

- *Stay quiet when the other person is talking.* This is obvious but so many people are bad at it. Close your lips if you must to keep from saying anything. Let the other person talk.
- *Do not interrupt.* Even though you have a thought you don't want to lose, do not interrupt. If you do, you demonstrate that you weren't listening to her anyway because you were deep in thought about some other issue you just had to blurt out.
- *Look in the direction of the other person.* In some cultures, it is appropriate to make eye contact; in other cultures, you only look in the general direction of the person. In both cases, it's not appropriate to stare. This is not an interrogation. A soft gaze in the other person's direction is a good strategy.
- *Stay on topic.* Whether you follow up on the person's point with additional ideas or answer questions, make sure you stay on

topic. If you quickly change the topic without a transition, she will assume you were thinking about something else while she was talking.

- *Use key words.* When you are unclear about what the other person has said, repeat some of his key words. You won't look silly; you will demonstrate you were listening.
- *Paraphrase.* When you think you understand what the person is saying in the context of the entire conversation, summarize what you've heard. This is a great way to let the other person know you are listening. Caution: Be sure not to do this too often in a conversation, because you will look like either you are trying too hard or you are mimicking the speaker.

Active listening is a core networking and image-building skill. Just because you may know how to actively listen doesn't mean you actually do it. Put these rules into continuous practice in every conversation. Think back on your last few conversations. Which of these rules could you have applied? Use these guidelines as part of your Job Spa image refresh and revitalization.

JOB SPA BONUS CHALLENGE

In your next few conversations, see how long you can actively listen without interjecting your own opinion or perspective or changing the topic.

Put It All Together

Congratulations on completing the third week of your Job Spa. You have identified what you want to get out of your Job Spa experience, recognized ways to improve how you are working on your current projects, looked at ways to grow your network, and put a plan in place!

Now it is time to put ideas into action. Here is your calendar for the week. Before you get ready for a well-deserved weekend, think back on the week. What went well? What did you learn? What do you want to work on or accomplish next week?

Congratulations on completing your third Job Spa week!

JOB SPA TREAT *for the* WEEK

Have lunch with a nonwork friend.

Calendar for Week (3) Day (1) 2 3 4 5

Time	Action	Notes
6:00 A.M.		
7:00 A.M.		
8:00 A.M.		
9:00 A.M.		
10:00 A.M.		
11:00 A.M.		
12:00 P.M.		
1:00 P.M.		
2:00 P.M.		
3:00 P.M.		
4:00 P.M.		
5:00 P.M.		
6:00 P.M.		
7:00 P.M.		

REMINDERS

- Create realistic milestones for your Job Spa goal(s).
- Create and update your task list.
- Grow your network.
- Practice your active-listening skills.

Calendar for Week (3) Day 1 (2) 3 4 5

Time	Action	Notes
6:00 A.M.		
7:00 A.M.		
8:00 A.M.		
9:00 A.M.		
10:00 A.M.		
11:00 A.M.		
12:00 P.M.		
1:00 P.M.		
2:00 P.M.		
3:00 P.M.		
4:00 P.M.		
5:00 P.M.		
6:00 P.M.		
7:00 P.M.		

Calendar for Week (3) Day 1 2 (3) 4 5

Time	Action	Notes
6:00 A.M.		
7:00 A.M.		
8:00 A.M.		
9:00 A.M.		
10:00 A.M.		
11:00 A.M.		
12:00 P.M.		
1:00 P.M.		
2:00 P.M.		
3:00 P.M.		
4:00 P.M.		
5:00 P.M.		
6:00 P.M.		
7:00 P.M.		

Calendar for Week 3 Day 1 2 3 4 5

Time	Action	Notes
6:00 A.M.		
7:00 A.M.		
8:00 A.M.		
9:00 A.M.		
10:00 A.M.		
11:00 A.M.		
12:00 P.M.		
1:00 P.M.		
2:00 P.M.		
3:00 P.M.		
4:00 P.M.		
5:00 P.M.		
6:00 P.M.		
7:00 P.M.		

Calendar for Week (3) Day 1 2 3 4 (5)

Time	Action	Notes
6:00 A.M.		
7:00 A.M.		
8:00 A.M.		
9:00 A.M.		
10:00 A.M.		
11:00 A.M.		
12:00 P.M.		
1:00 P.M.		
2:00 P.M.		
3:00 P.M.		
4:00 P.M.		
5:00 P.M.		
6:00 P.M.		
7:00 P.M.		

week four
SHARE YOUR PLAN

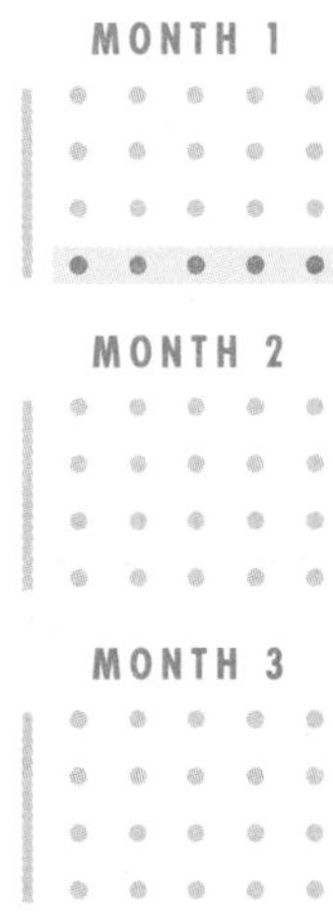

"Luckily last week I was able to find time on my manager's calendar to meet. When we meet, I am going to share my Job Spa plans and get her input and insight. It's kind of funny; I am actually excited to have this meeting. I'm looking forward to letting her know that I am taking initiative. I'm proposing ideas for a couple of projects. One of the projects I want to initiate is a new customer-intake process. I noticed that if we change a couple of steps in how we interact with our customers, we can create a better experience for them and save time. I also want to create a customer-satisfaction survey that gives us more information that we can really use, which is something I have never done before.

"I scheduled a couple of lunches with a few teammates for this week to get their input and see if they know anyone else I should talk to regarding some of my plans. Maybe they would like to work with me on these new projects? I'm feeling optimistic and excited about my plans and at the same time I want to make sure that I have enough time in the day to get everything done. Although my plans aren't a huge shift from what I am currently doing, I am now clear on what is important to me and that feels really good."

Welcome to Week Four!

By now you have a plan in place and are ready to get going. But before you embrace the complete Job Spa experience, check to make sure you are ready for your transformation. In this week, share your plans with coworkers and your manager. This is important because it allows people to see your new commitment to the company and yourself. They can also provide their insight, additional information, and confirm that your plans are working well.

In addition to sharing your plans, continue to build your active-listening skills by practicing the art of asking, informing, and making clear requests. These skills will benefit you tremendously this week and beyond as you share your plans and gather input. Also in this week, think ahead to ensure you are effectively managing your time by preparing for the unexpected. Last, stay on the path to Job Spa bliss by gathering and developing the knowledge you need.

WEEK 4	JOB SPA REGIMEN: GET CONFIRMATION
GOALS	Confirm your plans with your manager and coworkers.
TIME	Review your time habits and plan for interruptions.
KNOWLEDGE	Confirm that you have the right knowledge, or know where to gather the knowledge you need.
TEAM	Get feedback, buy-in, and support to move forward.
IMAGE	Practice asking, informing, and making clear requests.

Goal

Up to this point, your Job Spa has centered on your specific activities: What do *you* want? What is *your* commitment? What are *your* goals? Now it's time to turn your attention in a new direction: your manager. Who? Your manager may be your best friend, nemesis, or a complete stranger. Whatever the case, it's time to seek her out, sit her down, share your plans, and most important, get her support.

The Big Kahuna

One of the most important concepts critical to your success is "managing your manager."You mean you get to manage your manager? Absolutely. It's a must. As counterintuitive as that may sound, every manager's dream and underlying expectation is that you will be one step ahead of him when it comes to your work. The goal for any evolved manager is to have a direct report who is a mind reader . . . one he doesn't have to manage.

Beyond demonstrating you are on top of things, managing your manager also ensures that you are not living the myth that your manager is your mommy or daddy and will take care of you. You are self-sufficient, you think ahead, and you take initiative; you do not need handholding. The key is to understand your manager's communication preferences. Managing your manager is an important practice to keep up, especially as you share your plans this week.

Caring and Sharing

Last week we walked through the planning process and explored the importance of defining the resources you need to reach your goals. In addition to building or reinforcing the love between you and your manager, there are some other very important reasons to meet with her. Your goal is to share, confirm, and get her support for your plan. Why? Consider the following:

1. Your manager is the gateway between you and the paycheck (okay, that's an important and obvious one).
2. Your manager is the gatekeeper charged with allocating funds for the resources you need (fine, that will make life easier).
3. Your manager will want to know that your newfound sense of freshness and your coinciding objectives are aligned with what she needs you to do as part of your job.
4. Simply put, you will want to have your manager's support.

Schedule a meeting with your manager to review your plans. Start off with the objectives and ideas that relate to your current role and responsibilities. Begin with "I have some ideas about my current projects, and I would like your insight. I also want to talk with you about some additional things I am thinking about." Build the case for what is in it for her and how she, the team, and your projects will benefit. Allay any of her additional concerns by demonstrating that you have thought through your plans.

My Manager, Jeff (aka the Great Satan)

Okay, so maybe, just maybe you are one of those unlucky individuals with a boss who has developed his management style tormenting souls in the eighteenth level of Hell. Fear not. You will still need to have the conversation regarding your new goals and objectives. What becomes imperative is that you will need to first confirm your current work-related projects, share ideas on how to improve this current work, then share any complementary objectives.

Warning: Consider the boss from hell's perspective. He is probably easily intimidated or insecure, may not want to help you, or simply may not like you. If this is the case, you probably don't want to share new plans that entail getting a promotion that will take you away from your current department or any plan that doesn't involve your current day-to-day job. Continue to tread carefully.

Consider the following steps in the case that Jeff *is* your reality:

1. Share your plans with Jeff. Your opening line could be, "I've been thinking about my current projects, and I have some ideas that I think will help them succeed even more. I want to get your input."
2. Make it all about Jeff. Find a way to link your objectives to his larger goal, the department's goals, and even the company's goals.
3. Keep your larger end goal (i.e., promotion or leaving the department to go work for someone you don't consider Satan) to your-

self. There is no point in creating an environment that is more uncomfortable.

4. Use your discretion about what and how much you share.

There's Something I've Never Asked You

Have you ever actually asked your manager about his communication preferences? Or, have you just made the assumption that what you have always done is what he wants? As part of your 100 Percent Commitment, it's time to pull back the curtain and ask some important questions.

So what questions should you ask? Think about it as the top ten things your manager wants you to know about how to successfully work with him. This includes pet peeves and preferences. Pet peeves can include dislikes such as writing e-mails in all lower-case letters. For preferences, define the following:

- When you have updates, does he prefer e-mail, voice mail, one-on-one meetings, or staff meetings? What is his preference for the frequency of updates? How much detail does he prefer?
- When you need feedback on documents and completed work, does he prefer e-mail or meetings? How often does he want to give you feedback?
- When you have requests, does he prefer e-mail, voice mail, or meetings?
- When you have emergencies, what is the best way to reach him? What does he consider an emergency?

Although you've worked together for some time, even the boss from hell will appreciate that you have taken the time and effort to better understand how he likes things done. When you understand what keeps your manager up at night, you are better equipped to prioritize your work effectively, make him look good, make his life easier, and most important, make *your* life easier.

JOB SPA BONUS CHALLENGE

Identify the three actions you can take to begin managing your manager.

Time

As you ease into your fourth week in your Job Spa, differentiate between activities that support your 100 Percent Commitment and those that don't. Keeping current projects on track, delivering on daily demands, and staying focused on larger objectives is a challenge. Conquering this challenge requires taking your time-management artistry to a new level.

Right Place, Right Time

Self-examination time! Be honest. What have you noticed over the past decade and more specifically in the past several weeks about how you manage your time? How are those routines treating you? Are you managing your time effectively? Or are you stressed out every morning as you sit in traffic and hope no one notices you're late for the 9 A.M. staff meeting? It's time to break the cycle.

Review your time-management skills to make sure you get to your appointments on time. In fact, try something even better: Get to your destinations five minutes early. Imagine the benefits of arriving five minutes early to each meeting. You will have more time to get settled, and you'll be less stressed. This also gives you a few moments of quiet time to do the following:

- Think about what you want to get out of the meeting (i.e., goal setting).
- Think about your next task for the day.
- Organize your task list.
- Catch up on some notes or e-mail (if you carry your laptop or PDA with you).

Think about it: You could be more productive *and* effective by being early!

Think back through the past three weeks. Have you been early, on time, or late? You are forgiven. Let's move forward. What do you want your timing to be in the next eight weeks of Job Spa and beyond? When do you want to arrive at work and to meetings? What time do you want to be home by? How tight do you want your deadlines?

Some people like procrastination and the adrenaline rush it brings. While that may be okay for you, make sure it does not impact anyone else. Even though you think you are doing fine by delivering just in time, your coworker may have a different perspective and a bad case of nervous indigestion. Consider the consequences of the reputation you develop. If others find out you like to procrastinate, they may be less forgiving for future appointment or deadline blunders. Think about how your time-management skills are supporting your ability to deliver your 100 Percent Commitment.

Stubborn Like a Mule

While procrastinators may abound in office environments, there is also another type of person and behavior that is also less than desirable. Some folks freak out at any changes to their schedule. If this sounds a tad familiar, it's time for some tough love: Get over it! You are not *that* important in the corporate scheme of things. Change happens all the time, and it has nothing to do with you. As part of your Job Spa, limber up and move with the flow.

The key to success in any company is your ability to bend and flex with change. Change will likely impact your life, schedule, goals, milestones, deadlines, and task list. Change may not always be fun and can take you by surprise. But hey, you only live once. The rush of a surprise every now and then can keep you on your toes. Too much change, however, can be overbearing and lead to burnout. Understand how you react and manage change. This will help you become more adept and psychologically prepared.

As you think about your adaptability to the minor and major changes that have occurred in your personal and professional life, consider the following:

- What was your typical reaction? Defensive, angry, excited, or optimistic?
- Are there certain types of changes that cause you to react in a certain way?
- What reactions would have been more useful?
- Given the themes you are noticing, what do you want to commit to doing differently?
- How will you remind yourself to keep your reactions productive in upcoming situations?

Your ability to manage your reaction to change will go a long way to help you become successful in your job. When you can effectively anticipate, manage, and evolve with change, you are better prepared to move in the right direction and be a leader. Become more flexible, keep your cool, get less stressed, and focus on productively adapting to the change.

Plan for Disruptions

Plan for disruptions and interruptions. Sound counterintuitive? It *is*. How can you plan for something unexpected? By making sure you have ample time to do your work. You have strategically created slack in your schedule so when a surprise enters your world, you can make accommodations.

Distractions are everywhere. It is up to you to be discriminating about what, when, and how you divert your focus from your well-planned schedule. It may be very hard to avoid further inquiry when you hear the news that the vice president of Pharmaceuticals got caught sampling *way* too much of the product. However, you may need to exert some self-discipline if you are distracted by the need to play fantasy football and keep up with your friend, using Instant Messaging.

We live in a world where there are so many distractions that it takes discipline to stay focused on the task at hand. Part of maximizing your time is having the restraint to focus on and complete specific tasks within a defined time frame. As you work on an item, don't bounce between answering the phone, responding to e-mails, and surfing the latest headlines. By maintaining a singular focus, you'll find you actually complete your task faster. Your commitment manifests itself through your ability to cut through the noise. Are you listening? So stop scratching the abnormally fascinating bump on your forearm and pay attention.

Aside from the traditional social, biological, and technical distractions, you will find that unforeseen work issues may divert your focus. The effective time manager can quickly adapt. First, validate that what has come before you is a priority concern. Second, identify a course of action. No matter the priority of the surprise, communicate to applicable parties how you will respond. (Clue: High priority surprise = Your manager needs you to review and update an important report before 9 A.M. the next day.)

JOB SPA BONUS CHALLENGE

Identify and practice two new time-management behaviors.

Knowledge

Last week as part of your Job Spa, you began to quench your thirst for knowledge by identifying what information you needed as part of your Job Spa objectives. In this week you will take another gulp to review what you know and additional information you will need.

Gap Analysis

The first step to define what you need is to perform a knowledge-gap analysis. What is a gap analysis? It is not an analysis of the space between your ears. In the context of your goals, a gap analysis identifies the skills, information, and knowledge required. To perform a knowledge-gap analysis, break it down. Define your overall job responsibilities and your Job Spa objectives. For each project or objective, define the following:

- What information do you need to achieve each of your goals?
- What information do you currently have?
- What information will you need to acquire?

Types of Resources

So many objectives . . . so little time. As you've begun to notice from your gap analysis, you may need lots of different kinds of information. The required information can vary from simple to complex. There are four different levels on which you can organize this information to help you develop a comprehensive plan to complete your tasks, acquire resources, and develop your skills:

1. *Archival information:* This is a quick hit of information that you can research on your own to develop an understanding in a particular subject area. This includes books, articles, research papers, and information available on the Internet.
2. *People information:* This information and knowledge resides in someone else's experience or expertise. To access this type of information, first determine who these individuals are, make contact with them, and then retrieve the information. Because the information is coming from people, it is dynamic (not static like archival information). There are more variables such as accessibility, biases, and willingness to share that may also impact the kind of information you can retrieve and the time it takes to get it.
3. *Training:* This is a formal process by which you develop or increase your knowledge base and skills. Training can be in the form of courses available through books, online, or in classroom settings. Training requires time and will usually vary from several hours to multiple days.
4. *Certification and degree programs:* An even deeper level of information and knowledge acquisition is through completion of a program in which there are governing bodies, specific requirements, and exams that ensure you know the information. This may take longer to complete than training because there are credentials associated with these types of programs.

Use these four levels of knowledge resources to get clear about the kind of information you need to successfully complete your current projects and Job Spa goals. More often than not, the sources of information and knowledge you need for your current projects, enhancement ideas, and new projects can be found in the first two levels. Make sure you update your Job Spa plans based on any new information that you have identified, including impact to budget.

JOB SPA BONUS CHALLENGE

Identify the knowledge you need in each of the four levels and take action.

Team

In keeping with the spirit of Job Spa, you must check in with a few trusted coworkers to confirm your plans. They will have a valuable perspective on what you want to achieve and maybe even some fresh ideas. Even though you may not realize it, your colleagues are vast storehouses of information. All it takes to tap into this intellectual gold mine is asking the right questions—or a free lunch.

Feed a Coworker, Gather Some Information

Your head is a great place to germinate new ideas. However, your trusted coworkers can provide invaluable perspective on how and why your ideas will thrive or need revision. Identify a few who will give you straight answers, are trustworthy not to include their personal agenda, and have resources that will help you succeed (review your gap analysis, if need be). Take each one to lunch at a different time. Use them as a sounding board for your ideas, plans, and perspective.

So this all sounds great on paper . . . but what if they don't want to share their honest reactions? Perhaps you are concerned that even the ones you *like* may not have your best interests in mind? One of the potential challenges of the funny farm called your workplace is the disconnection between the words *team player* and the manifestation of team player behavior. You want to avoid walking into a piranha pool slathered in steak sauce.

Be sensitive to how your teammates might perceive you. Instead of announcing big Job Spa plans with the utmost enthusiasm and confidence, use a little small-talk lube to get the conversation started (think rapport building). Don't just jump in and drop the bomb of how this book has changed your life and now that you have this 100 Percent Commitment, you are driven in a whole new way. This will freak them out and send them running for the hills. Ask how they are doing. Then introduce what you are working on as part of your Job Spa and tell them that you value their input (yes, stroke their egos a little as long as it's the truth). Get their insight on your plans, alternatives, ideas, and recommendations for specific next steps or additional people you need to meet.

JOB SPA BONUS CHALLENGE

Schedule lunch with a coworker each day of this week.

Image

Aren't meetings great! Nowhere else can people spend an entire day under the guise of "working" and get absolutely nothing accomplished. Remember your last meeting? You were talking, others were talking, and you thought you were listening. Only to realize fifteen minutes after the end of the meeting that you can't remember what was said by anyone. In retrospect, people were talking over each other, and no one was truly listening. Everyone was just waiting his turn (or not) to state his opinion. Do your part to increase meeting effectiveness and support your image. Deploy your honed and toned communication skills.

In this section, build upon your listening skills from Week Three. Refine your ability to ask questions and state your opinions. We will also spend time on phone and e-mail communication etiquette.

Back and Forth

Think back to the last great conversation you had . . . and no, we don't mean the one you had after two glasses of wine. Specifically, think about the last great *work* conversation you had. It may have been in a staff meeting or a one-on-one meeting with a colleague. More than likely, it was a conversation in which your views and opinions were taken seriously and perhaps you learned something from others as well. It was a conversation that felt equitable. The other person probably walked away with the similar feelings. So what made it so great?

Ideally, a conversation is an exchange of questions, opinions, and statements of fact. The art of effective conversation is a fluid display of each party's opinion and genuine curiosity. This often does not happen in the workplace. Most people are too busy to ask for your thoughts and simply make requests or bark their opinion. This method of communication is often frustrating. The result is a residue of unsaid or poorly exchanged thoughts and information. Fortunately, you can control how you engage with others. You can influence how others communicate with you.

Effective conversations are a balance of asking questions and stating opinions or sharing facts: asking and informing (adapted from Peter Senge, *The Fifth Discipline*, New York: Doubleday, 1990). The nature of a relationship determines the sequencing of opinions and questions. As stated earlier in the Goal section on managing your boss, you first want to state your opinion, and then invite questions. Your boss is expecting you to tell her your recommendations on how to solve an issue.

When working with peers, it is important to start off by asking their opinion and then state your own. The rationale is the same as when you and another come upon a doorway at the same time. It is polite to let the other person go first. In the case of peers, you do not want to alienate them or look as if you are upstaging them. You are not just asking them for their opinion to be polite. The information you get might change your opinion or redirect your initial inquiry.

If you have direct reports, make sure to ask for their opinions first. Due to power dynamics (i.e., you are the authority figure), you want them to openly give their opinion without being intimidated.

Often you will find yourself in conversations with others who may be a bit stunted in their communication aptitude. Perhaps you may have a manager who can only give orders or a coworker who seems to talk forever without making a point. No matter the situation, your objective is always to be professional. In tough situations, ask probing questions to get clarity. Once you get enough information, leave the situation as quickly as possible. If needed, check your sanity with a trusted coworker or colleague outside the company.

Make Clear Requests

Remember when you were twelve years old? You hinted at wanting an upgraded video-game player for your birthday and instead got a book? Not quite what you wanted, you mumbled as you tossed the book in the back of your closet, never to be seen again. Yes, sometimes in life, hints don't get heard. In the workplace, you cannot afford to have this happen. Subtle hints may not be enough. Communicating who you are and what you need for your success requires clarity and confidence.

The objective of making clear requests is to ensure that you are effectively communicating what you need to the people around you. Being up-front may not be the easiest communication skill to develop. Many people avoid confrontation or are not comfortable at the thought of asking for things from others. An effective request is polite and thoughtful, and communicates not only the specifics of your request but why you are making the request.

Effective requests require a balance between humility and boldness. For those of you who never learned to ask for things, it's time to practice. Finding your voice and articulating what you need is critical to your career success. On the other end of the spectrum, if you are one of those individuals who are not shy about asking and are perhaps even a little demanding, you may want to soften your tone.

When you make a request, have these components in mind:

WHO are you asking? In team meetings, you may throw out a request, everyone agrees it's a good idea, and no one owns the idea.

- *Poor example:* "How about if we got additional data for our client?"
- *Strong example:* "Ramona, will you get additional data for our client?"

WHAT exactly are you asking? You may be clear on what you want, but are you being as explicit as possible?

- *Strong example:* "Ramona, will you get additional data for our client?"
- *Stronger example:* "Ramona, will you get the last five years' net and gross revenues for our client?"

WHEN exactly do you need the information? You may think the situation is urgent, while the other person has no idea you are waiting for him. Be clear on what the time frame is.

- *Strong example:* "Ramona, will you get the last five years' net and gross revenues for our client?"

- *Stronger example:* "Ramona, will you get the last five years' net and gross revenues for our client by Tuesday?"

E-mail and Phone Etiquette

We have been talking about how to bring your 100 Percent Commitment to life through verbal (i.e., asking questions and stating your opinion) and nonverbal communication (i.e., dress code). A tremendous amount of communication takes place virtually, either over the phone or via e-mail or text messaging. Although virtual communication can speed the communication process, there are also some potential pitfalls. As a part of your refreshing Job Spa, let's give your e-mail and phone etiquette a thorough exfoliation.

- *Don't answer the phone if you can't talk* (yes, we know you do that). If the call goes into voice mail, the caller understands that you are either unavailable or not at your desk.
- *Don't talk too loudly.* Whether you are in your cubicle, office, or on your cell phone, speak at a moderate volume. It is inconsiderate to assume that your conversation is so important that it needs to be broadcast to everyone within twenty feet.
- *Leave concise and clear messages.* Two minutes is way too long to listen to a voice mail. However, cryptic messages, such as, "It's me, call me," do not provide the other person with information or increase the likelihood she will return your call. State who you are, the nature of your call, and where you can be reached.
- *Follow up within twenty-four hours.* When someone leaves you a voice mail, get back to him even if it is to acknowledge that you will address the issue at a later time.

You have time to think about your response before hitting the Send button. Take it. Because e-mail is written communication, it serves as documentation of a conversation. In many instances this can work to your advantage for future reference and later reading.

In other instances, it can be a huge source of embarrassment if it is passed around by colleagues.

Don't create your own language. Keep your text-messaging code for casual interactions with your buddies off the job. Your boss is not going to be happy deciphering "aamof@teotd aeap rx." (Translation: "As a matter of fact, at the end of the day or as early as possible.")

Here are some further guidelines:

- *When drafting an e-mail, double-check your grammar and spelling.* Most e-mail systems have a spell-check program. Re-read your e-mail twice if you are in a hurry and three times, if you're not, to make sure you catch everything before you send it. Read it slowly and out loud if you have a tendency to make a lot of mistakes.
- *Wait, calm down, delete, or edit angry e-mails.* E-mails produced in a swirl of annoyance or anger will come back to haunt you. Anger will show up in the tone of your e-mail. Never use all capital letters, which is annoying to read. It also indicates you are upset and out of control. This is not appropriate in a professional environment. If in doubt, get a perspective check from a trusted colleague who can read through a draft and tell you if your tone or wording is harsh or inappropriate.
- *Don't send e-mails at 11 P.M.* Many corporate employees have been regular recipients of the "look at me I am still working at night" e-mail. Unless it is in conjunction with a project or deadline, such an e-mail generally fails to impress. If anything, unless you work an alternative schedule, it demonstrates poor time management and a need for a life outside work. It may even look as if you are creating busywork, which raises the question of what you are doing during the daytime when you should be working.
- *Follow up within twenty-four hours.* Similar to voice mail, it is important that you get back to people promptly; if you cannot complete their request, give them a projected time when you'll do so. This process also ensures that you do not get behind on e-mail. It is very easy to go from 100 e-mails daily to 500 by week's end if you are not keeping up.

How you communicate with others sets the stage for how you are perceived. To help you attain your Job Spa goals, there is nothing more important than ensuring that what and how you communicate supports the image you want to project.

JOB SPA BONUS CHALLENGE

Practice asking and informing in your next conversation.

Put It All Together

Before you move on to your seaweed scrub, let's ensure you put everything into practice. You've done a gap analysis to identify additional information and knowledge you need to reach your Job Spa goals. You've gotten input from trusted coworkers about your Job Spa goals. You've shared your goals appropriately with your manager and asked for what you need. Now it is time to put ideas into action.

Here is your calendar for the week. Plug in what you need to do in Week Four to get your ideas on paper and the details documented. Before you get ready for a well-deserved weekend, think back on the week. What went well? What did you learn? What do you want to work on or accomplish next week?

Congratulations on completing your fourth Job Spa week!

JOB SPA TREAT *for the* WEEK

Play and get inspired by your favorite song on your way to work.

Calendar for Week (4) Day (1) 2 3 4 5

Time	Action	Notes
6:00 A.M.		
7:00 A.M.		
8:00 A.M.		
9:00 A.M.		
10:00 A.M.		
11:00 A.M.		
12:00 P.M.		
1:00 P.M.		
2:00 P.M.		
3:00 P.M.		
4:00 P.M.		
5:00 P.M.		
6:00 P.M.		
7:00 P.M.		

REMINDERS

- Get input regarding your Job Spa goals from trusted coworkers.
- Practice managing your manager.
- Practice clearly asking for what you need.
- Manage your calendar and plan for disruptions.
- Share your Job Spa goal with your manager.

Calendar for Week (4) Day 1 (2) 3 4 5

Time	Action	Notes
6:00 A.M.		
7:00 A.M.		
8:00 A.M.		
9:00 A.M.		
10:00 A.M.		
11:00 A.M.		
12:00 P.M.		
1:00 P.M.		
2:00 P.M.		
3:00 P.M.		
4:00 P.M.		
5:00 P.M.		
6:00 P.M.		
7:00 P.M.		

Calendar for Week (4) Day 1 2 (3) 4 5

Time	Action	Notes
6:00 A.M.		
7:00 A.M.		
8:00 A.M.		
9:00 A.M.		
10:00 A.M.		
11:00 A.M.		
12:00 P.M.		
1:00 P.M.		
2:00 P.M.		
3:00 P.M.		
4:00 P.M.		
5:00 P.M.		
6:00 P.M.		
7:00 P.M.		

Calendar for Week (4) Day 1 2 3 (4) 5

Time	Action	Notes
6:00 A.M.		
7:00 A.M.		
8:00 A.M.		
9:00 A.M.		
10:00 A.M.		
11:00 A.M.		
12:00 P.M.		
1:00 P.M.		
2:00 P.M.		
3:00 P.M.		
4:00 P.M.		
5:00 P.M.		
6:00 P.M.		
7:00 P.M.		

Calendar for Week (4) Day 1 2 3 4 (5)

Time	Action	Notes
6:00 A.M.		
7:00 A.M.		
8:00 A.M.		
9:00 A.M.		
10:00 A.M.		
11:00 A.M.		
12:00 P.M.		
1:00 P.M.		
2:00 P.M.		
3:00 P.M.		
4:00 P.M.		
5:00 P.M.		
6:00 P.M.		
7:00 P.M.		

week five
LAUNCH

"Last week there were a couple of surprises. The first surprise was that my manager was impressed that I had really thought out my plan and was clear on where I needed help. She really liked my ideas about the customer intake process, and she loved the idea of a different kind of customer survey. She even agreed to my request for the company to pay for a survey design class. That asking and informing stuff really works!

"The second surprise was a bit of a bummer. I met with John who has been a teammate for a year. When I told him my plans, he seemed surprised and hesitated when I asked him for help to connect me with a VP he's working with. This interaction made me think about how I come across. Was he concerned I might embarrass him? Or did he feel he didn't know me well enough to feel comfortable introducing us? Or did I make him feel competitive? It was a reminder to consider how I want to be perceived by my coworkers. Maybe I need to reach out to them more often to solidify our relationship.

"Now that I have the green light to move forward on the project, I am going to make sure I get out and connect with coworkers to build stronger relationships. I also need to think further about what information is required for the projects and people I will need to include."

Welcome to Week Five!

Let's crank up the heat. Now that you've prepped over the last month, it's time to move from the mud bath to the sauna. This week you will formally launch your plans. And of course, it wouldn't be a week at your Job Spa if you didn't continue to tweak and adjust those subtle yet crucial professional skills.

As you work toward implementing your plans and achieving your goals, stay on track by continually developing your skills and honing your company savvy. This is a good time to take a closer look at your company's time-management practices and patterns. Compare your time-management patterns with theirs to ensure that you are in sync.

As you open your implementation chakras, you are also going to identify knowledge-development opportunities. What do you want to be known for at work and how will you make sure that your message gets across to those who matter?

WEEK 5	JOB SPA REGIMEN: IMPLEMENTATION
GOALS	Meet and greet.
TIME	Compare your time-management patterns to your company's.
KNOWLEDGE	Start getting the knowledge you need.
TEAM	Compare yourself to others on the team who are strong team players and identify what you can do differently.
IMAGE	Develop your PR message.

Goal

Often when you meet someone, it turns out that you have a mutual friend. It is speculated that there are six degrees of separation between you and every other person on the planet. That's right, all that separates you and the person who cut you off in traffic this morning are six other people. Think about that the next time you cut off that old Granny standing in line, she might be Grandpa's new girlfriend.

Moving a bit closer to your world of work, the number of connections between you and everyone else at work is even smaller. Imagine how few coworkers separate you from everyone else in your company? Probably not too many! A big part of your Job Spa is recalibrating expectations and refreshing your skills. An additional area of "refreshment" includes your network. In previous weeks, you took time to define your current network. Your goal for Week Five is to ensure that you continue to build your network and identify opportunities for expansion and improvement.

Who Do You Know?

In Weeks Two and Three, you assessed your network to see who you know and determine who else you should be meeting. What steps have you taken over the past three weeks to expand your network?

To recap:

- Level 1 is made up of your direct contacts.
- Level 2 is made up of friends of friends (they know of you).
- Level 3 is composed of people with whom you do not have a relationship at all and only know of the person through indirect relationships.

There is no quota for how many people are needed to make a network effective. However, we recommend (Are you listening, Introverts?) that you have a network that contains more than one person. Humor aside, determine the current strength of your network:

- Given your 100 Percent Commitment and correlating Job Spa objectives, what would you like your network to help you achieve?

- How many teammates and coworkers have you met in the past four weeks?
- How many times have you spoken with these people?
- How many people in and out of work can you call upon for assistance and information?
- What areas of expertise or resources do the people in your network have to share?
- Who else do you need to meet in your company?
- Who else do you need to meet or reconnect with outside your company?

Unfulfilled Obligations

After you have defined what a stronger network looks like, turn your plans into actions. Start with the network you currently have. Make sure you are taking the time to properly care for and nurture these relationships. It's easier to strengthen an existing relationship than to build one from scratch. It is also easier to use the people in your immediate network to expand your number of relationships than to connect with total strangers.

First, refresh and reconnect with your existing network by following up on any unfulfilled obligations. Sometimes things fall between the cracks during busy times. In the rush of getting your project done two weeks ago, did you forget to send Maria that phone number? It is time to catch up on any past-due obligations, follow-through, and reinforce your relationships.

Next, follow up with colleagues or those who have provided assistance. You know, the "important but not top priority" list. For instance, that thank-you phone call you owe to Billy Joe for his time a couple of weeks ago when he took an hour to explain the science of dry-erase markers. Don't let these things linger. A follow-up "thank you" will leave a good impression with others and keep the door open to future collaboration.

If you really want to seal the deal and strengthen your relationships, think about what you can proactively provide the people in your network. Didn't you come across a great article last week on the hybrid of dry-erase pens and erasers that is taking the office supply industry by storm? Billy Joe would love to read about that! Always be on the lookout for things that you can share with the people in your network.

JOB SPA BONUS CHALLENGE

Reconnect with three people with whom you haven't had contact for more than six months.

Time

Speedy like shiatsu or slow and peaceful like a hot stone massage, your work environment has a pace all its own. Be aware of whether the folks around you seem to scurry around like psycho chipmunks or seem to match the pace of old-growth redwoods. It is very important to watch the pace of your work environment, how time is treated in your company, and how you compare. The last thing you want is to get nicknames like "turtle" or the large-quad-shot non-fat-no-whip-mocha speed freak. To be effective and embrace your 100 Percent Commitment, it is important to understand and move with the pace of your environment.

Time Has a Life of Its Own

Confirm your understanding of the value placed on deadlines and schedules. Differentiating between what people say they want and what actually happens will help you plan, prioritize, and successfully navigate through the logistical irregularities in your company. For example, meetings are set to begin at the top of the hour and everyone says it's important that meetings start on time, and yet if you actually arrive on time, you will be sitting there alone for a good five minutes. Now everyone purposely shows up five minutes late. How do these issues affect your current behaviors and work habits?

The same rationale holds for behaviors related to deadlines. Are they steadfast or flexible? What are the effects of this? In general, what you do notice about how coworkers meet deadlines and respond to e-mail and phone messages? Do people respond promptly? Are there explicit rules such as a twenty-four-hour turnaround? Having a clearer understanding of how time is treated will also provide the opportunity for you to influence and be a role model for more professional behaviors such as starting meetings on time, meeting communicated deadlines, and responding promptly (within twenty-four hours) to incoming e-mail and voice mail. Your awareness and role-modeling of the right practices will help you to be more effective in fulfilling your 100 Percent Commitment.

Break out the radar. Answer the following: Is the pace in my company intense or laid-back? What about your company makes it this way? For instance, is work requested from you today expected to be done immediately, or are deadlines amorphous and open? Based upon your 100 Percent Commitment and related Job Spa goals, adjust your own speed to be in sync.

Pace is one element of your environment that you have probably been subconsciously aware of yet have not explicitly analyzed and used to your advantage. Making the effort to understand the influences and impact of time will help you manage your time more effectively and use time to your benefit.

Time and the Bigger Picture

Let's take a step back and look at the influence of time on your company and industry. Take a look at your company's strategy. Is it focused on long-, short-, or medium-term objectives? Look at how your company is planning on reaching these objectives. Some companies focus on a short-term, fast-growth strategy, while others focus on longer-term, steady growth.

The impact and influence of time will vary depending on the industry. For example, a drug company may take ten years to get a product to market while a software company takes two years to develop a new version of its product. Regardless, it is important to understand the correlation of time to current strategy, planning, and broader organization objectives. If your company is focused only on the immediate pressures of today, it may be missing a number of opportunities that will require longer-range planning. This may be an opportunity for you to think through bigger ideas and recommendations. At a minimum, understanding your company's industry, influences, and pace, and how it compares to its competition will help you see the broader picture and how you play a part in it.

JOB SPA BONUS CHALLENGE

Define the pace of your company's industry and consider its impact on your company and your profession.

Last week you inventoried your current knowledge and identified additional knowledge, skills, and resources you will need. It's time to get tactical: prioritize and start your research, make contacts, and move into action.

X Marks the Spot

Launch your quest on sure footing by thinking through and prioritizing which information or source you need to hit up first. Based on your plans, maybe it's time to sign up for that training class because it is only offered once a year and it fills up fast. Prioritize which coworkers need to be contacted first. Given your earlier reflections on time and pace, consider about how quickly or slowly they will get back to you. It may take a while before you get the information you need. So plan accordingly and communicate to the people who are relying on you.

Play the Matchmaker

As you gather your new horde of knowledge, keep in mind how what you are learning can be shared and utilized by your coworkers, team, and company. For example, if you are taking a training program, capture the key learning points and present them at a staff meeting. Draft a white paper or summary document if you are initiating research as part of your job. Look for opportunities to connect people you've met. Consider this question: As you develop your network, how can you leverage and expand your network by taking an active role to connect people? You will be seen as well connected, in "the know," and a valuable company resource.

"Will it seem as if I'm trying too hard, especially if I've never done this before?" you ask. Not if there is a meaningful connection to be made. The emphasis is on *meaningful.* Try connecting a couple of coworkers and see how it goes. In later weeks you'll have an opportunity to review how your coworkers received your knowledge-sharing techniques.

JOB SPA BONUS CHALLENGE

Identify two coworkers with whom you can connect.

Team

In Week One of your Job Spa, you gathered feedback from your manager and some trusted colleagues. Last week you tapped them to get their support and insight on your Job Spa objectives. This week as you launch your plans, continue to evolve your team player aptitude. Step back and examine your coworkers to get a better sense of the behaviors that reinforce camaraderie and group effectiveness.

It's What Makes Your Team Unique

Each team has a unique set of dynamics and culture. During your tenure with your team, you have probably observed a variety of traits or characteristics, such as underlying team politics, what is important to the team, and how work gets accomplished.

Define the unique behaviors and attitudes of the individuals on your team and your team as a whole. This will help you more effectively influence and implement your plan. The intent here is to exercise a little team player aikido to use the team's underlying forces to your advantage.

Some questions to consider include:

- Do teammates share equally with every member or only with specific individuals?
- What are the personality dynamics among your teammates?
- Do certain people have more or less influence, and why?
- What are the underlying assumptions or expectations between team members around sharing and collaboration?
- What are the explicit (stated) and implicit (not stated but expected) roles of the team members?
- How is your team perceived by the outside world?

Based on your responses, how can you form stronger team relationships? How can you get your team to help you be more successful in achieving your Job Spa goals? Shift a few behaviors to get more connected to your team, and open up room for more collaboration.

Values? What Values?

Most companies have identified a set of corporate values. Your company is probably no different. Sometimes these values become an integrated part of the way the company conducts business. Other times the list of corporate values is nothing more than a neglected poster tucked away in a desk drawer. Does your team have a set of values that it follows?

Understanding the explicit and implicit values of your team will ensure that you are maximizing your effort as a true team player. Are your team's behaviors consistent with these stated values? Have these values been forgotten? Do you need to rehydrate them into vital, healthy, everyday practices? Here's your chance.

Mean What You Say

There should be no confusion and misunderstanding when it comes to communication. Ensure your message has meaning and clarity. Here's an example: "I will send you that information ASAP." Two possible translations: "You will have that information in the next hour," or "You will have that information whenever I remember to send it your way." Depending on the person or the company, that sentence can mean a number of different things.

Dig deeper into the specifics of team behavior. Refresh yourself as to how teammates and other coworkers make and follow through on commitments. Are you the image of credibility and follow-through? Do people provide you the information in the time you requested? Do people meet deadlines and keep to schedules? Here's another opportunity to role-model your 100 Percent Commitment and demonstrate effective collaborative or team-oriented behaviors. Conversely, avoid the behaviors that undermine collaboration and group success. This is a great time to consider what team-related behaviors you want to change or improve.

Blame Game or Accountability

Observe how the people on your team hold themselves accountable. If someone drops the ball, does he take every action necessary to keep you informed? Or does he point the finger at others and say it's their fault? Worst yet, does he simply disappear? In your work with others, do you take responsibility for mistakes? Are there things you do that undermine your 100 Percent Commitment? The sign of a strong team is commitment, communication, and accountability.

Cube Wars

Humans can be territorial creatures. In conjunction with your observations of team behavior, take a peek at how coworkers share information and protect their resources. In some companies, departments undermine each other, compete for resources, and refuse to collaborate. Although this may sound less like corporate America and more like urban gang warfare, turf-guarding is common in many companies. Maybe you have seen this firsthand or maybe you are guilty of a little turf-guarding.

How can you spot turf-guarding? Turf-guarding symptoms may include reluctance to share information, tightly controlling valuable resources, and refusal to collaborate with other groups. Typically, people guard their territory for fear of losing resources, control, or credibility. It is a natural reaction, albeit counterproductive.

If you find yourself in a situation with a colleague who is clearly turf-guarding, find out her concerns and navigate carefully. Alleviate coworker paranoia by careful stroking of the ego and expressing well-placed compliments. Give credit to others in front of management. If you come up against intense turf-guarding that prevents you from getting the resources you need, call in air support. Involve a member of the management team to quickly resolve the issue.

If, on the other hand, you recognize that you have gone over to the dark side and have become a relentless turf-guarder, do not fear. There is hope. As part of your 100 Percent Commitment, look at what you can give to others. Letting go can be risky, especially in an organization where turf-guarding is epidemic. How else are you going to break the vicious cycle except to lead by example? Here are some steps you can take to get that warm, fuzzy feeling that comes from sharing and to ensure that you get credit for your accomplishments:

DO IT IN PUBLIC. Volunteer information and resources in a group setting.

MARK YOUR TERRITORY. Put your name and information in the footer and document settings.

ASK FOR CREDIT. If you have created a body of research or original work, make sure you communicate to others that this is your work and it is important that you are cited in order to ensure consistency.

Be a Trail Blazer

Did you read the preceding paragraphs and chuckle that collaboration in your team is less like synchronized swimming and more like anarchy at the preschooler's wading pool? Dysfunction happens, and luckily, these are the moments where your 100 Percent Commitment is put to the test. Weaker office drones have taken the easy route and joined in the maddening spiral. However, you have the choice to identify the behaviors that you want to demonstrate and directly or indirectly influence others.

JOB SPA BONUS CHALLENGE

Identify two behaviors you want to role-model in your interactions with your team or coworkers.

Image

How you are perceived today at your company began the moment you started your job. Intentionally or unintentionally, you have continued to reinforce this image. Whether how you are perceived is right, wrong, justified, or unjustified is no longer important. Now you must align how you want to be perceived with how others see you.

Maybe things got off to a rocky start. Perhaps you can do a better job communicating your skills. Maybe you want your manager to think of you as the person to turn to when things get rough. It is never too late to reaffirm the good and recast yourself in a new light. Remember the myth that your hard work and loyalty will get recognized? Don't leave your image and recognition to the gods of fortune. It's time to go to the Image Salon and create your PR message.

Craft Your Message

The intent of your PR message is to communicate your *values* and how you want to be known. This is your opportunity to craft and launch your own advertising campaign. Think back to the Volvo example in the User Instruction chapter. These cars are synonymous with safety. They are designed and marketed with that intent. The ad campaigns contain visual depictions of safety belts, airbags, and other contributors to safety performance. The word associations in Volvo's ad campaigns are also all about safety.

Now switch from Volvo to you. What do you think when you think of yourself? What do you want others to think when they think of you? You want to send a consistent message through what you say and do. You may not have airbags and five-point seat belts, but you have other high-performance features. As you craft and deliver your message, always consider the five *W*s: why, what, who, when, and where.

Why do this? The intent of your PR message is to communicate your values and what you want people to know. This is the embodiment of your 100 Percent Commitment.

What do you want to be known for? Find three key words or phrases that represent that image. Consider what you want to give to your job. What about what you want to take from your job? What is your professional legacy? What are some key words or phrases that best capture this information? Once you have determined them, deliver this message to others. Think deeds *and* words. Remember, your actions must be consistent with your words. Say you want to be known for being reliable. If you tell a coworker, "I'll get you the document by tomorrow," and then you don't deliver—you've just undermined your message. Align your behavior with your message.

Who are the three target markets of your PR messages: your manager, teammates, and coworkers? You should have a desired PR result for each target.

When do you want to share? All day, every day. You should always be prepared to stealthily deploy your PR message when the moment is right. Keep in mind that your message has to be relevant to the topic being discussed. Suddenly exclaiming that you value collaboration and want your team to have all the resources it needs is great—except for the fact that Bob only wanted to know if you wanted cream in your coffee.

Where do you want to share? Every conversation is an opportunity to deliver your PR message. Every e-mail, every face-to-face conversation, every phone call, and every meeting are opportunities to communicate your message and reinforce your desired image.

Deliver Your Message

State each of your PR messages in one concise sentence. Rotate your PR message depending on the situation. Your goal is to convey your message three times to three people within three months (remember, that's a minimum requirement). Don't bombard others with your message; do it frequently enough to get it across. Think stealth versus shock and awe. There is a balance between subtlety and obnoxiousness.

Finally, in addition to your behavior, make sure your physical appearance is consistent with your message. This includes how you groom and present yourself as well as your body language. As we've discussed, communication is a package deal composed of much more than the words that come out of your mouth. Look in the mirror to take advantage of your Job Spa by freshening up your wardrobe and appearance.

JOB SPA BONUS CHALLENGE

Communicate one element of what you want to be known for in your next e-mail or meeting.

Put It All Together

Congratulations on completing the fifth week of your Job Spa. Let's put all these great ideas from this week into practice.

You've thought about what a successful network looks like. Get out there and keep networking. You've gotten clear about how your company and team treat time. Now it's time to speed up or slow down (depending on what's most appropriate for you). You've thought about how to truly become a team player, and it's time to let go of the past and move forward to build stronger connections with your coworkers. Finally, get clear on what you want to be known for, and go out there and say it and do it!

Here is your calendar for the week. Plug in what you need to do in Week Five to get your ideas into action.

Before you get ready for a well-deserved weekend, think back on the week. What went well? What did you learn? What do you want to work on or accomplish next week?

Congratulations on completing your fifth Job Spa week!

JOB SPA TREAT *for the* WEEK

This weekend, do something for you such as getting a massage, getting a manicure/pedicure, playing golf, going on a hike, or going for a bike ride.

Calendar for Week (5) Day (1) 2 3 4 5

Time	Action	Notes
6:00 A.M.		
7:00 A.M.		
8:00 A.M.		
9:00 A.M.		
10:00 A.M.		
11:00 A.M.		
12:00 P.M.		
1:00 P.M.		
2:00 P.M.		
3:00 P.M.		
4:00 P.M.		
5:00 P.M.		
6:00 P.M.		
7:00 P.M.		

REMINDERS

- Get your PR plan into place and start communicating.
- Keep networking and play matchmaker.
- Adjust your pace to be more successful.
- Role-model your 100 Percent Commitment.

Calendar for Week (5) Day 1 (2) 3 4 5

Time	Action	Notes
6:00 A.M.		
7:00 A.M.		
8:00 A.M.		
9:00 A.M.		
10:00 A.M.		
11:00 A.M.		
12:00 P.M.		
1:00 P.M.		
2:00 P.M.		
3:00 P.M.		
4:00 P.M.		
5:00 P.M.		
6:00 P.M.		
7:00 P.M.		

Calendar for Week (5) Day 1 2 (3) 4 5

Time	Action	Notes
6:00 A.M.		
7:00 A.M.		
8:00 A.M.		
9:00 A.M.		
10:00 A.M.		
11:00 A.M.		
12:00 P.M.		
1:00 P.M.		
2:00 P.M.		
3:00 P.M.		
4:00 P.M.		
5:00 P.M.		
6:00 P.M.		
7:00 P.M.		

Calendar for **Week (5) Day** 1 2 3 **(4)** 5

Time	*Action*	*Notes*
6:00 A.M.		
7:00 A.M.		
8:00 A.M.		
9:00 A.M.		
10:00 A.M.		
11:00 A.M.		
12:00 P.M.		
1:00 P.M.		
2:00 P.M.		
3:00 P.M.		
4:00 P.M.		
5:00 P.M.		
6:00 P.M.		
7:00 P.M.		

Calendar for Week (5) Day 1 2 3 4 (5)

Time	Action	Notes
6:00 A.M.		
7:00 A.M.		
8:00 A.M.		
9:00 A.M.		
10:00 A.M.		
11:00 A.M.		
12:00 P.M.		
1:00 P.M.		
2:00 P.M.		
3:00 P.M.		
4:00 P.M.		
5:00 P.M.		
6:00 P.M.		
7:00 P.M.		

week six
GET TRACTION

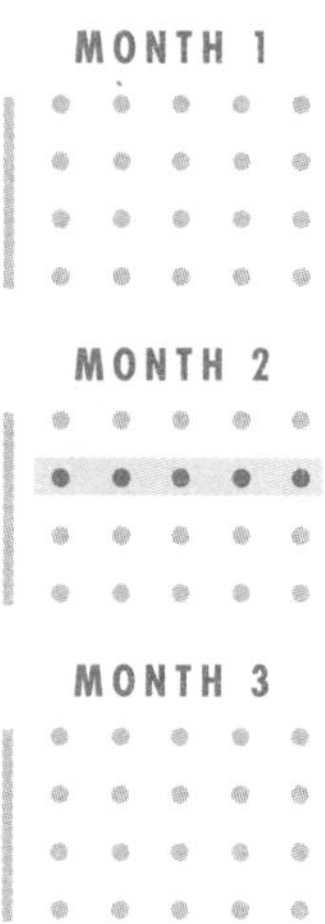

"I can't believe I'm already halfway through my Job Spa treatment! I can't wait to start practicing my PR message—all these years and I finally have my own PR plan. Looking back on the past five weeks, I feel really good about my progress. The commitment I made at the beginning of my Job Spa treatment is holding strong.

Looking toward the future and specifically the next six weeks, I want to make sure I balance my own needs to reach my Job Spa goals and continue reaching out to others. In the past I made an effort to share with coworkers my experience and new bits of information that came my way. Sometimes my information seemed to hit the mark, and other times, it didn't seem to go anywhere. I wonder if there is a better way to share and contribute what I know. If I'm going to make the effort, I've got to make sure that it's relevant and useful."

Welcome to Week Six!

It is the halfway point of your spa treatment and time to reflect on your experience. Fortify and replenish your energy for the path before you. The theme for the week is getting traction. You will scrub away the mud mask and take a look in the mirror to make sure the

100 Percent Commitment you made during Week One still reflects what you want. You will also maintain collaborative momentum by continuing to develop and practice relationship-building skills. Look for the most effective ways to contribute what you know to the people around you.

Over the previous six weeks, you have recalibrated your expectations. You have a better understanding of how you are perceived and want to be perceived. Your 100 Percent Commitment helped you get clear on what you want to give and take from your job. As a result, you created your Job Spa goals. You are now more focused on your direction, making the most of your experience, and aware of your surroundings. This is an important time to ensure that your plans are on track.

WEEK 6	JOB SPA REGIMEN: MAKE PROGRESS
GOALS	Revisit your 100 Percent Commitment.
TIME	Align your time practices.
KNOWLEDGE	Observe how information is shared.
TEAM	Identify opportunities to collaborate.
IMAGE	Build rapport.

Goal

It's the midway point in your Job Spa. You've scrubbed, cleaned, refreshed, and progressed. Over the last few weeks, you have identified and begun to work toward new objectives. Now that you have moved from words to actions, it's time to revisit the commitment you made back in Week One. Revisit your commitment to help you confirm what is working well, how your work environment is supportive or challenging, and what modifications you need to make in order to continue toward your Job Spa objectives.

More than anything else, the commitment you made in Week One was about making a choice for your success. You made the decision to consciously change your perspective, make the most of the opportunities around you, and build the discipline to set goals that have meaning. Take a step back to refresh and reinforce the commitment you made. Take a few moments to stop and consider your accomplishments in the past five weeks.

Minty Fresh or Time to Freshen Up?

As you review your 100 Percent Commitment, think for a moment about what is still important to you. The commitment that you made was comprised of two elements:

1. A new attitude toward your success
2. Implementing behaviors that embody your attitude

Over the past five weeks, you have in many ways started your job anew. As your new perspective has evolved, what is still important to you as part of your 100 Percent Commitment? Given the reality of your workplace and its receptiveness to your 100 Percent Commitment, what has stuck? What has vaporized? What do you want to change, based upon your experience?

Maybe before you started your Job Spa, your attitude was to do only as much as you needed despite your complaints to everyone in your family about how awful work was. There were no opportunities for advancement. With your Job Spa, you shifted your attitude to look at work as a place of abundance and opportunity. You looked for opportunities in addition to advancement. You realized that advancement was only part of a larger picture. Through your new Job Spa lens, you took initiative and developed skills that would ultimately make you more qualified for a bigger role.

What elements of your attitude and level of commitment do you want to keep? Which can you get rid of without undermining your 100 Percent Commitment? Note: it can be tempting to ignore certain elements of your commitment. Avoid temptation to loosen up your level of discipline. You're doing great! Now is the time when momentum builds upon all of the great things that you have been doing. This is the time to refine your strengths. The point of this exercise is to confirm what is critical as part of your commitment and what is superficial.

Beyond attitude, let's take a look at behaviors. How have your behaviors changed? What are you doing differently? Before beginning your Job Spa, did you roll your eyes during staff meetings when your coworker could never just get to the point? Did you have the reputation for going completely ballistic and breaking out in a fit of corporate Tourette's when things weren't going your way? Identify new behaviors that reinforce your commitment? Are there any behaviors you want to change? Finally, how has your work ethic changed? Are you more conscientious of deadlines? Do you look for opportunities to help others?

Take a mental inventory of your level of commitment and engagement. Consider the feedback that you gathered from your manager and coworkers your first and forth weeks of Job Spa. Oh, yeah . . . feedback. That's right! You took the time to gather the feedback. What did you hear that really stood out? What actions did you decide to take? Now is the time to refresh what you heard and incorporate and reinforce any needed changes.

Review this chart to refresh and confirm what you want to give and take:

YOUR 100 PERCENT COMMITMENT	
GIVE 100 PERCENT	**TAKE 100 PERCENT**
Your attention (be present)	Appropriate salary and benefits
Your strategic thinking skills	Appropriate job title
Your knowledge and perspective	Career development opportunities
Your insights on what can be improved or new opportunities	Stimulating work or projects
Positive and constructive attitude toward coworkers and the company (even if you may not agree with them)	Opportunities to learn new skills

YOUR 100 PERCENT COMMITMENT	
GIVE 100 PERCENT	TAKE 100 PERCENT
Opportunities to change or role-model what you don't like about your company or environment (as opposed to complain)	Opportunities to learn from coworkers
Follow through on commitments	Build relationships
Execute work on time and with top quality	Opportunities to travel
Appropriate amount of time to your job	Opportunities to try a new role

If the Going Gets Tough

We never said that your Job Spa would be easy—refreshing and cleansing, but never *easy*. Any kind of change can be a challenge. The decision you have made to shift your perspective about your job, to make every moment count toward something bigger, to get more and give more can be an amazing challenge. This is especially difficult if your work environment does not support your efforts. There is an uncomfortable possibility that some of your coworkers may feel intimidated by your choices. Maybe they feel that if you succeed, they fail. Perhaps you have a manager who is intimidated by your effort and drive to succeed. Over the past few weeks, your perception of your company's culture may have shifted from warm, soft, and fuzzy to teeth and claws. There is no magic potion for tackling the issues of a manager or teammates who are not supportive. However, there are three steps that you can take to mitigate these headaches:

1. *Get clear:* Identify the behavior you perceive as undermining or not supportive. The objective is to call out individuals who are undermining you so that you can address these concerns. This is not an invitation to release that deep-seeded paranoia or go on a witch hunt.
2. *Impact:* Identify whether the behavior directly impacts your work, projects, or commitment to your success. For example, does your

manager intentionally withhold resources that you need to complete your project or simply make annoying side comments? Do your teammates conveniently withhold information that directly impacts your projects despite being told to give you the information?

3. *Confront or ignore:* Based upon the impact of the behavior, you can ignore or confront the issue. Certain problems are better ignored because they are only temporary, a one-time event, petty jealousy, not worth the effort, or not politically savvy. However, critical issues and abusive situations must be addressed and, if needed, escalated to the appropriate people. No matter what, you do not deserve to be subjected to an emotional terrorist of a boss or an inappropriately competitive teammate.

If you decide to confront the problem, take these two steps:

1. *Gauge your relationship.* Consider if you can talk with your manager or teammate to provide gentle, direct feedback. Yes, you can provide feedback, even to your manager, if it's done constructively. This starts with an attitude of curiosity about the situation and your observations, not accusations. Remember your feedback skills: State your observations, the impact, and what you are asking for that's different (i.e., your request). As part of your request, demonstrate that you are open to being a part of the solution; inquire if there is something that you need to do differently.
2. *If you cannot communicate directly with this person, then you may need to escalate to a neutral party* (i.e., HR). Remember, only escalate after you've made a direct attempt to communicate what's not working and make an effective request. You don't have that many silver bullets. Use them wisely.

WE'RE NOT SUGGESTING you throw a twenty-pound chip on your shoulder and look for the slightest provocation from those who you think are not supportive. The last thing you want is to have is the reputation as the office psycho. What you are being asked to do is to identify where the danger zones are in your environment so that you can address these issues constructively.

Dispel the Myths

As part of revisiting your 100 Percent Commitment, take a look at the three workplace myths to ensure that you are no longer living in this mythical land. Conquer these deceptive and seductive sirens of the cube farm. Let's refresh so you know what to look for:

MYTH 1 *My boss/manager is my mommy or daddy and will take care of me*—Take initiative, identify opportunities, and manage your manager.
MYTH 2 *My hard work will always get recognized and rewarded*—Take accountability to communicate your strengths and contributions.
MYTH 3 *Company loyalty equals job security*—You need to create your own plan and career objectives.

Moving forward, identify what you need to do additionally to dispel these myths. As part of your Job Spa, continue to look for opportunities to take initiative, manage even the most unruly manager, and take accountability for your career success.

JOB SPA BONUS CHALLENGE

Review, confirm, or revise your special Job Spa goals.

Time

It's time for a little Job Spa time-management checkup. As you know, soaking in as much as you can from your Job Spa requires that you align your time-management skills. You have probably felt a slight, and at times not so slight, tension over the past weeks between the demands of work and what you want as part of your Job Spa. This week take a brief step back and reflect on what you are doing to ensure that you are managing your time and incorporating your time observations from last week (your pace versus the company pace).

Time for Me

To focus on this comparison exercise, block off a little "you" time. Schedule time in your calendar for reflection. If you can't find time during your office hours, make time before or after work. Find a place where you will not be distracted, and turn off the phone, yes, even your mobile phone. Explore the following questions:

1. How is your pace during the day? Are you frenetic or calm?
2. Are you successfully balancing your immediate responsibilities with the objectives you have set as a part of your Job Spa?
3. In what ways are your time-management skills impacting (positively or negatively) how you give and take 100 percent?
4. Are you maximizing your time-management tools and practices?
5. Are there changes you can make that will have a positive impact on how you manage your time?

After answering these questions, make the choice to do what's right for you and your 100 Percent Commitment.

JOB SPA BONUS CHALLENGE

Identify two things this week that will help you maximize your time.

Knowledge

One of the bigger Job Spa treatments has been exercising and massaging your gray matter to think through all that you know and need to know. Talk about a deep-tissue massage! As you reach out and connect with coworkers and sources and gather information, what have you noticed pertaining to sharing processes and protocols? Do you have access to the knowledge you need? The information in the following section will help you build upon what you already know about your team, coworkers, and company.

Heightened Awareness

If you have been on the job for a while, it's easy to take for granted the ways in which knowledge and information is shared. It's time to put on your Job Spa glasses to confirm the most effective ways to gather and share that information. Identify the standard procedures for sharing information at your company. What are people's preferences for what is shared over e-mail versus in meetings?

Additionally, how is information shared at different levels and groups in the organization? Do senior leaders in the company share information differently from midlevel management? Your attention to specific protocols and practices make you more effective. While you more than likely already know this at the subconscious level, the value of this exercise is to ensure you have explicit understanding of these various methods and do something about it.

The CIA (Corporate Intelligence Agent)

In every company there are people who are "in the know." They have the inside scoop about what is really happening. This is the kind of information that impacts your day-to-day activities, but no one tells anyone in a company-wide e-mail or during a team meeting. These informal sources of information can be critical conduits to getting the coveted insider's view of the company and how things really get done. In most companies, access to the juicy information is based on relationships and trust.

Like a dramatic spy novel, there are people among you who have corporate intelligence. Who are the people you work with who always seem to be in the know? Do you have a CIA? You know, that special person who is your go-to contact for the inside intelligence, whether it's finding out what really went down at the company picnic or getting the latest on the new product strategy. Don't stress if you have not identified or made a trusted relationship with an insider. Building these relationships takes time and requires building trust. If there is a specific "target" individual who is loosely connected to your network, continue to get closer and build trust with individuals who are directly connected to this person.

Sorry, We Don't Do That Here

Most living organisms have three primary responses to being exposed to new things: fight, flight, or acceptance. When introducing new ideas, companies are pretty much the same way: resist and attempt to vaporize the idea, ignore it and hope it goes away, or accept new ideas. How were your previous suggestions received? To ensure your new ideas that emerge from your 100 Percent Commitment don't scare the locals, understand how ideas are embraced. Think about your previous experience or observations. Moving forward, what steps can you take to maximize acceptance?

Notice how much information or time people need in order to adopt or try something new. Adjust your influencing skills accordingly to effectively build a case for your ideas. Depending upon the culture of your team and company, create a strategy for sharing information or initiating new ideas that reflects the culture (e.g., getting support from an influential person before offering up your idea to the group). Making your ideas readily digestible requires research and planning.

Although potentially time and strategy intensive, the right preparation can ensure that the path ahead is clear of messy obstacles.

Learning Organization or Repeat Offender

The key to effectively managing knowledge is to make sure what is learned from various projects is shared with the rest of the company. Continuing down our path of knowledge-management growth, confirm how knowledge from projects is shared so you are not reinventing the wheel.

First, look to see if there is a process for learning from earlier endeavors. Or do people hold on to the information without even thinking of how they can share? A postmortem (although a horrible-sounding term) is usually a great way most teams share the lessons learned? Does your team regularly do this? This reduces redundancies, inefficiencies, and possibly prevents costly future mistakes. Although this may sound intuitive and obvious, you might be surprised how many companies do not keep track of their knowledge and lessons learned.

Review your company's and team's practices for sharing this type of information. This is a great opportunity to demonstrate your 100 Percent Commitment if your company is not big in sharing previous project results and discoveries. This is your opportunity to initiate new practices and protocols for building upon previous work. Set an example by creating and sharing a one-page summary of a recent project identifying key points of experience, learning, or challenges.

Show Me the Money

As much as leaders say they value and support sharing knowledge, there may be very little sharing going on. Are people rewarded for sharing? Are there consequences for *not* sharing? Is sharing knowledge and resources role-modeled by leaders in your company?

What is the reality about sharing within your company? How can you effectively gather and share resources without ruffling any feathers? For example, if sharing knowledge is not a common practice in your company, take more time to explain why you are looking for information, what you plan on doing with it, and acknowledge the other person's contribution. In the next section, we will build upon the overall company practices for sharing.

JOB SPA BONUS CHALLENGE

Identify one new practice, idea, or tool that can help your company share more effectively.

Team

Occasionally we break from the usual workplace optimism to provide a bit of candid advice. As professionals who have balanced the importance of team effectiveness with anger management, we offer the following: Consider the development of your social skills as a strategic competency. The better your social skills, the more successful you will be. Because like them or not, coworkers are a part of your work life. So open your mind, remove any chips from your shoulder, and smile. At times there may be bitter pills you have to swallow. As you smile and take a gulp, remember that your colleagues will more than likely be providing input to your boss on your annual performance review. The ball is in your court.

As you have conversations with teammates and coworkers this week, focus on your team skills. Every interaction is an opportunity to demonstrate that you are the embodiment of the team player philosophy. This is true even if you are a closet introvert who would like nothing more than to be left in peace to enjoy the isolation tank that is your office.

Make the First Move

Look for opportunities to collaborate. For maximum 100 Percent Commitment points, take the initiative to share. Don't be shy. As we explored in the Goal section for this week, there may be individuals who are not your biggest fans. Guess what? This is an opportunity to build trust and proactively address any issues.

Why Share?

You've put a lot of time and effort into a project or initiative. You've done great research and really made sure you poked around to find out more about anticipated trends that will affect your idea. Wouldn't it be great if others could benefit from your hard work? That's what giving 100 percent is all about. "But what if others steal my idea?" This is a legitimate concern. Why would you want to give away your hard work? Here are five reasons:

1. You reinforce your 100 Percent Commitment.
2. You can be the first to claim the idea.
3. You reinforce to others that you are a valuable resource.
4. You confirm or test your assumptions.
5. You expand your discoveries by getting others' insight.

Can you think of more reasons to share?

What to Share

Now that you're clear on why you want to share, the next question is what exactly do you share? Interrupting your staff meeting to share your thesis on why sheep herding on the Tibetan plains was outlawed in 1765 may seem incredibly fascinating—to you! However, your coworkers just might have a second opinion. Share information that is relevant. You probably learned some interesting things and developed some new insights while pursuing your Job Spa goals. Share what you discovered in the process of creating and pursuing your plans, information that might be valuable to your team. What opportunities exist for your team or coworkers? You want the people around you to know you are thinking and looking ahead.

What if someone steals your ideas? As mentioned earlier, this can be a risk. Think through what your boundaries are between sharing enough so that you provide value and not feeling vulnerable to theft. Following through on your 100 Percent Commitment has everything to do with taking the initiative and being forward thinking. Don't operate from a place of fear and let the chance to be a star pass because of all the what-if conversations that float in your mind. Job Spa is about taking and creating opportunities.

How to Share

Err on the side of signs of intelligent life. Assume your coworkers are intelligent. When you share, use an approach that inspires a conversation with your audience as opposed to a lecture. This way, you get the conversation going. Teammates will jump in, ask questions, and may even add their two cents, which could spark a new idea. This is the essence of innovation. Here are guidelines for how to share:

- *Timely:* The information must be timely. If you share it two weeks after the fact, the relevance and value of what you are providing may have diminished.

- *Relevant:* The information must be relevant to others and what they are currently working on or will be working on.
- *Form:* Identify the most effective way to communicate information.
- *Format:* Consider what your audience will respond to. Some folks want cold hard numbers, others want an oral history of research and application, and still others want to hear what you have done pertaining to the topic.
- *Permission:* Ask others for permission to share. Give your teammates the opportunity to say yes or no. They will be much more open to receiving information from you when they have agreed to receiving this information.
- *Venue:* Determine how best to share the information. Should you do so in a personal meeting, phone call, e-mail, or by carrier pigeon? Depending on the type of information, consider the most appropriate method.
- *Confidentiality:* Use discretion and the guidelines of your company.

At the end of the conversation, ask if this information was helpful. You want to open yourself up for feedback. It's the best way to learn what additional resources *would* be helpful and how best to communicate with your audience.

Now What?

Now that you have poured your heart and soul into sharing with your team, what do you (and they) do with the information? Here are some different paths:

- What you shared led to exploring new perspectives and inspired others on the team to think in different ways. You've broadened their perspectives.
- What you shared helped confirm people's beliefs in the direction of their work and perspectives. They know they are on the right track with their own projects and goals.

- What you shared inspired conversation and provided you with new information that has either confirmed your current goals or prompted you to look at some different options to support your Job Spa objectives.
- Whatever the outcome, sharing this information with your team demonstrated that you are interested in making a contribution.

JOB SPA BONUS CHALLENGE

Identify and share at least one work- or project-related item of value to your team or coworkers.

Image

As part of refreshing and confirming your 100 Percent Commitment, take a closer look at *how* to build relationships and communicate with your coworkers. In this section you will hone practical skills to quickly create a connection with new colleagues and get back into the groove with longtime associates. It's time to focus on how to create rapport. As a pillar of relationship-building acumen, developing and mastering your rapport-building skills will take practice. However, you will quickly notice the benefits of having rapport skills once they're integrated into your interpersonal repertoire. Imagine all the relationship-building qualities of a communal mud bath without the mess.

Why Bother?

You might think you already have the silver-tongued skills and all the workplace connections you will ever need. Think again. Your 100 Percent Commitment requires you to constantly expand the boundaries of your network. Building and honing your rapport-building skills will give you the tools to ensure that you are effortlessly expanding your connections and delivering your PR message with fluidity.

Rapport is the process by which a common connection or understanding is created between two individuals. Through creating rapport, you form an initial level of trust, facilitating ease of conversation and exchange of information. Rapport can be established through identification of commonalities such as professional or personal interests, shared opinions or views (i.e., relationship rapport), or through more subtle elements such as the creation of a connection and being in sync with the other person through similar speech patterns or body language (i.e., behavioral rapport).

Relationship Rapport

Relationship rapport is creating common ground with someone new or simply knowing someone for a long time. In every interaction, you can be more effective if you can quickly establish common ground. That means asking questions to better understand the other person and in return sharing appropriate personal information to create a connection. Peppering an unsuspecting coworker with a series of questions without volunteering your information will not build rapport and will probably just annoy her.

With new people, ask general questions that focus on discovering commonalities: where the person lives, previous work experience, family, and hobbies. Be sure to ask questions that cannot be answered by a yes or no. Open-ended questions allow for sharing more information that will help build the relationship. With people you already know, ask questions that reconnect you and continue to build upon the relationship.

Behavioral Rapport

Establishing common interests or similarities is only one aspect of rapport. The second aspect is behavioral rapport, which comes from the field of neurolinguistic programming (NLP). No, you will not be brainwashed. Although behavioral rapport has its roots in various disciplines of psychology, it's an effective way to quickly build trust at a very instinctual level. Besides, you do this naturally anyway, but most of the time you aren't aware of it.

Here's some background: NLP started in the 1960s in Santa Cruz, California, based on the research of Richard Bandler and John Grinder. The findings were interesting and applicable to anyone. Bandler and Grinder noticed that when therapists matched their clients' verbal and nonverbal communication patterns, they were able to quickly establish trust.

How is this relevant to you? Have you ever felt in sync with someone? For some reason, you both naturally mirrored one another. If you videotaped the interaction, you probably would have noticed that your body language looked similar to each other. When you waved your arm with excitement, the other person did the same. You probably even started to sound like the other person. You used the same key words: They said, "No way!" and you responded, "Yes way!" even though that's not something you would normally say.

You were probably both talking faster and louder because you were having such a great time. Boy, that was a fun conversation! And yes, you were in behavioral rapport. This happens when two people are in sync, whether they have known each other for a long time or just met. That's what helped these therapists in the study establish trust so quickly. They were able to get in sync with their clients.

Back to the example: If you were to ask the other person later why she felt comfortable, she might tell you that you made good eye contact, listened, and asked good questions. While you were doing all these things as part of your active listening skills, you were also demonstrating in your behavior that you were similar to her and therefore not a threat.

So what are the implications for the workplace? Well, you can take the chance and hope that you are in sync with another person. Or you can increase the likelihood that you are in sync by purposely *mirroring* the other person. We don't mean mimic. An exact duplication is too contrived. General similarities are good enough. Most people will not even notice that you are doing this. As far as they are concerned, the conversation just feels good. The small percentages who do notice are usually delighted to see you make the effort.

Behavioral Rapport in Action

Regardless of the history of the relationship (i.e., relationship rapport), the critical times to employ behavioral rapport are at the beginning of the conversation to create a sense of familiarity and comfort, and during the conversation if differences in opinion arise. In both cases, your intent is to first create comfort/trust and then to engage or re-engage the person in the conversation as needed. If he is upset, you will probably need to re-engage him and reaffirm that you can be trusted.

For example: When someone is upset, most people try to calm the person by demonstrating the exact opposite behavior. A person who is upset may point his finger, have a furrowed brow, raise his voice, and use harsh language. Trying to calm him by acting calmly is the exact opposite behavior. This is a clear mismatch and the opposite of building behavioral rapport. In fact, the person who is upset will feel misunderstood if not patronized. This tends to upset him even more. You end up having an ever-escalating situation.

To demonstrate that you understand his emotional state, you must match and pace the other person before you proceed. Based on this example, to build behavioral rapport with someone who is upset, you too might raise your voice slightly, use similar body language to get his attention, and say forcefully that you understand he is upset. While this may seem like a lot to do to effectively engage with someone, it works and will become easier with practice. The key here is to verbally acknowledge the person's point (don't argue) and mirror him. This will get his attention and re-engage him.

Behaviors to Match

As you get into sync with the other person, focus your attention on the following four areas:

1. External behavior (what you see)
2. Internal behavior (how the other person is feeling)
3. Voice (tone and pace)
4. Language (phrases and specific words)

When you match external behavior, notice the other person's body language. This includes her posture, hand gestures, and facial expressions. Posture is important to match. Some people like to lean forward in the conversation and others like to lean back in their chair. Make sure you match the other person's posture as this particular behavior conveys a lot of information regarding how she is feeling. If the other person is leaning forward and you are leaning back, she might think you are not interested in the conversation.

"But I feel comfortable sitting with my arms crossed and leaning back in my chair." It does not matter what your intent was. It's what the other person perceives and therefore is *the* truth in her mind. So get out of your comfort zone and try out new postures.

You may notice that some people have a tendency to use more hand gestures. If that is the case, try moving your hands more. At first this may feel uncomfortable, but remember no one knows you are trying this out. The same goes with facial expressions; if you find the other person smiles a lot, do the same.

Match internal behavior if you need to deeply empathize with the person and are finding it difficult to connect. Put yourself in her shoes. What does it mean that she is sad right now? What do you think her being sad feels like? She may feel down, pessimistic, or distracted and unable to focus on her work. When you can match her at the deeper level of emotion, you can more easily understand what she is experiencing. At that point, you operate from a more informed place when it comes to the decisions you make and how you choose to communicate with this person. You may decide to postpone the conversation if she is too emotional or distracted. Or you may decide to express your empathy. When you match the other person's internal state you demonstrate that you understand why she feels a certain way.

Match the other person's voice quality. Pay attention to the other person's tone and speed. Think about it in the context of being at the library. When you burst out in a loud conversation with your friend, you are not surprised by the nasty look you get from the librarian who reminds you to use your "library voice." So you adjust accordingly. You lower your voice and talk a little slower. This is no different when you are matching another person to get into behavioral rapport with her.

How fast is the other person talking? Compare yourself to her. Do you need to speed up or slow down? Think about the last time you had a conversation with someone who spoke as slowly as molasses. Do you remember that feeling of irritation when you tried to get through the conversation quickly and he just didn't finish what he had to say? This is a clear pacing mismatch. Monitor how fast the other person talks, so you can adjust your pace to establish and stay in rapport.

Your tone of voice conveys a lot of information. If you roll your eyes and sarcastically say, "What a *great* idea!" people will know from your body language and tone that you are not in favor of it. Or think about the time someone greeted you unenthusiastically. Boy, didn't you know she was not happy to see you? Tone of voice is a huge indicator of someone's internal state. It provides additional clues to identify where the person is emotionally and how to best approach her. You will also need to consider your own voice tone to ensure you are sending the message you intend. So get comfortable with adjusting your tone and speed.

Finally, pay attention to the key words or phrases used in your conversations. The same words can have different meaning for different people. To create behavioral rapport, it is important to use the other person's key words and phrases. Ask for clarification if they use words that may have multiple meanings. You can easily damage behavioral rapport if you make an incorrect interpretation. It's safer to stick to exact words. Have you ever had the experience of paraphrasing and when you got it wrong, it made the situation even worse? Not only did the person you were talking to feel irritated, she also got the sense that you didn't get what she was trying to say.

Becoming adept at rapport building, both in the moment with behavioral rapport and long term with relationship rapport will help you fit into new environments and strengthen existing relationships. Rapport away!

JOB SPA BONUS CHALLENGE

Identify one rapport-building trait that you will practice in your next conversation.

Put It All Together

Congratulations on completing the sixth week of your Job Spa. Before you move on to your mud bath, let's ensure you put everything into practice.

This week you've been getting traction on your Job Spa objectives. Revisit your commitment to yourself to ensure that you are energized and fortified for the remainder of your spa. Share, share, and share some more! You may even have some tough conversations this week regarding your observations of others' support levels. Remember to come from a place of curiosity and try to understand your coworkers' point of view by asking lots of questions instead of assuming they have a negative intent toward you. Use your rapport-building skills.

Here is your calendar for the week. Plug in what you need to do in Week Six to get your ideas into action.

Before you get ready for a well-deserved weekend, think back on the week. What went well? What did you learn? What do you want to work on or accomplish next week?

Congratulations on completing your sixth Job Spa week!

JOB SPA TREAT *for the* WEEK

Get outside, bask in the daylight, and take a walk during lunch.

Calendar for Week (6) Day (1) 2 3 4 5

Time	*Action*	*Notes*
6:00 A.M.		
7:00 A.M.		
8:00 A.M.		
9:00 A.M.		
10:00 A.M.		
11:00 A.M.		
12:00 P.M.		
1:00 P.M.		
2:00 P.M.		
3:00 P.M.		
4:00 P.M.		
5:00 P.M.		
6:00 P.M.		
7:00 P.M.		

REMINDERS

- Get recommitted to your 100 Percent Commitment.
- Get your routine, calendar, and task list organized.
- Give 100 percent to your team.
- Network and practice relationship and behavioral rapport.

Calendar for Week (6) Day 1 (2) 3 4 5

Time	Action	Notes
6:00 A.M.		
7:00 A.M.		
8:00 A.M.		
9:00 A.M.		
10:00 A.M.		
11:00 A.M.		
12:00 P.M.		
1:00 P.M.		
2:00 P.M.		
3:00 P.M.		
4:00 P.M.		
5:00 P.M.		
6:00 P.M.		
7:00 P.M.		

Calendar for Week (6) Day 1 2 (3) 4 5

Time	Action	Notes
6:00 A.M.		
7:00 A.M.		
8:00 A.M.		
9:00 A.M.		
10:00 A.M.		
11:00 A.M.		
12:00 P.M.		
1:00 P.M.		
2:00 P.M.		
3:00 P.M.		
4:00 P.M.		
5:00 P.M.		
6:00 P.M.		
7:00 P.M.		

Calendar for Week (6) Day 1 2 3 (4) 5

Time	Action	Notes
6:00 A.M.		
7:00 A.M.		
8:00 A.M.		
9:00 A.M.		
10:00 A.M.		
11:00 A.M.		
12:00 P.M.		
1:00 P.M.		
2:00 P.M.		
3:00 P.M.		
4:00 P.M.		
5:00 P.M.		
6:00 P.M.		
7:00 P.M.		

Calendar for Week (6) Day 1 2 3 4 (5)

Time	Action	Notes
6:00 A.M.		
7:00 A.M.		
8:00 A.M.		
9:00 A.M.		
10:00 A.M.		
11:00 A.M.		
12:00 P.M.		
1:00 P.M.		
2:00 P.M.		
3:00 P.M.		
4:00 P.M.		
5:00 P.M.		
6:00 P.M.		
7:00 P.M.		

week seven
GAIN MOMENTUM

"Last week I spent a few minutes reviewing the commitment I made in the first week. My commitment to give and take as much as I can is as strong as ever. This commitment has changed how I see my job, coworkers, and career. In reviewing my goals I realized that there is an opportunity to take what I am learning about changing the customer intake process into the realm of how we sell our services. One of my new goals is to share what we are learning with the sales team. One neat benefit of the work I'm doing is that I've been able to help build a project team that's working really well together. I have never led a project before, let alone assembled and led a team! I am learning more everyday about who I am and my potential.

"I am feeling really good about my progress and direction. My attitude seems to show because my manager made the observation that I look and sound more focused and directed.

"I need to remind myself to continually reinforce and expand my network. I wonder if John is free for lunch next week. It would be good to reconnect with him given our last interaction."

Welcome to Week Seven!

Last week you revisited, revised, and strengthened your 100 Percent Commitment. You are dialed in and on track to Job Spa success. As you cross over into the second half of your Job Spa, you are feeling energized. Use this energy to build momentum on your Job Spa goals. Review and update your goals and plans based on last week's commitment review. To ensure that you are keeping pace with your networking activities, incorporate some easy time-management techniques into your day. To sustain your momentum, do a quick pulse check of your network and use coaching skills to ensure it is strong and healthy. You're doing great!

WEEK 7	JOB SPA REGIMEN: REVIEW YOUR PROGRESS AND REINFORCE YOUR PLANS
GOALS	Make any changes to your goals and plans based on the review of your commitment last week.
TIME	Allocate time for networking.
KNOWLEDGE	Based on your confirmation or revisions to your commitment, identify any content, information, or knowledge worth sharing.
TEAM	Use coaching to strengthen relationships on your team.
IMAGE	Review and revise your PR plan.

Goal

Last week you made a 100 Percent Commitment pit stop. You are reinvigorated and refocused. It's time to keep going and align your actions and activities to what you want to achieve. While you're at it, this is a great time to review how your Job Spa objectives are shaping up and apply some project management mojo. Successful project management is a combination of planning, implementation, and realigning your plans to your target.

Do the Double Check

Identify any changes to your commitment or coinciding steps that you want to take to support your progress. For instance, you may have realized last week that despite your 100 Percent Commitment, you were still rushing out of work without taking a few minutes to review and prepare for the next day. Sticking to your "leaving work routine" can make a big difference in preparing for the next day. What actions do you want to take to support your 100 Percent Commitment? Now is a great time to turn those *aha*s into results.

Check Your Milestones

As you stroll down the path toward Job Spa destiny, look down every now and then to ensure that your path is clearly defined. Pull out your plan. Take a few minutes to look at the milestones in your plan. Do they line up to your objectives or do they need some tweaking? Effective goal-setters ensure they are on course by regularly reviewing their milestones.

As you work on your projects with excitement and enthusiasm, you may realize that there is added project complexity or less clarity. Are there any additional steps or bits of complexity that need to be addressed? Scan your milestones to see if you need to add more details or collapse multiple milestones. Consider any changes to the resources required to accomplish each milestone. New or modified milestones might require different resources.

Scope Creep

Think back to the last time you agreed to help friends move. You assumed that they would be packed by moving day. You showed up and realized that they hadn't done very much. What started out as helping people move turned into helping them pack, move, and then unpack. The job kept growing, and your blood pressure rose along with it. You didn't have the heart to say no at this point. Your friends needed you, but you're never going to let them forget it.

Well, make sure that your projects and Job Spa objectives do not suffer a similar fate. Often you'll find yourself in the middle of a project that you thought had a clearly defined destination, goals, and measures of success only to realize you are adrift in a sea of ambiguity. Welcome to scope creep. Things might have seemed clear just days ago, but now you have a queasy feeling that the project you have come to know and love has changed. Your Job Spa objectives and projects have been tainted with something else!

Consequences of scope creep can range from seemingly mild ambiguity to severe loss of direction. The good news is that if caught early on, scope creep is curable. So don't panic if you are in the midst of increasingly vague goals and additional objectives that don't relate to the project's initial desired result. It's not too late to get back to your original plans of improving customer satisfaction, which have turned into a massive project involving a reorganization of the whole department! Or maybe that Job Spa goal you set a few weeks back just needs a little clarity to renew its sparkle.

Here are some tips to avoid the *creep* and course-correct if you find that things are getting fuzzy.

GET A HEALTHY START. Have clearly defined goals from the start (as a Job Spa expert, you know this). Define objectives, resource requirements, and potential obstacles in advance. Consider prior experiences and causes for what took projects off course. If scope creep is an ongoing problem on your team or in your company, you may need to take the initiative to make sure that the right pieces are in place.

TRUST YOUR GUT. Don't ignore that bloated sensation as you start feeling that your project is growing larger. Only weeks ago it was such a cute little project, and now you can barely squeeze it into your calendar. Take a moment to think through how the size, scope, and deliverables might have changed. What are the implications of these changes to the potential for your objective's success? Identify the core of your objectives and shed elements that are not imperative. Communicate your observations that the original objective appears to be changing.

ADJUST ACCORDINGLY. Scope creep is often a sign of project or objective natural growth. Your healthy toddler of an objective has just outgrown its project plan and needs a bit of adjustment. If you find that is the case, modify your plan and account for any required resources. You will quickly find balance and serenity once you adjust your plan.

A common yet sneaky cause of scope creep is when other projects move into your project's orbit and glom onto it. These add-ons are often orphan initiatives that were either abandoned, never quite got off the ground, or were never formally completed. As adorable as these orphan initiatives can be, once they attach themselves to your projects, they can become burdensome parasites. So keep your eyes open. Stay clear of any project managers looking to ditch some project baggage that might distract you from your trajectory. Maintaining a laser-like focus on your destination will help you differentiate between valid additions to your objective or an orphan looking for a home.

Moving Target

More than likely you have a range of Job Spa objectives. Balancing and prioritizing these objectives requires that you keep track of how you or your environment is changing. Changes are expected. What you want can change, project priorities can shift, or your company may move in a completely new direction. In light of this, one of the most important things that you can do is to understand how these changes impact your plans, and as needed, communicate these changes.

It's time to play the squeaky wheel. Speak up and share your observations that changes are underfoot and could impact your objectives. This is especially critical if your objectives involve coworkers or related initiatives. What's great about raising your hand is that you gain two benefits. First, you intervene early in terms of scope creep. Second, you demonstrate to your colleagues that you are engaged and taking the initiative.

Now do not run around screaming bloody murder about the offending change and point an accusatory finger at the first person you can find—tempting as this might be. Instead, inquire politely that you thought you were expected to deliver *X* and now it looks like *Y*. Is that an accurate assessment? Odds are you will hear a collective sigh of relief that you took the initiative to ask the question that was on everyone else's mind. If your destination has changed, go back and renegotiate your deadline dates and what you are expected to deliver.

JOB SPA BONUS CHALLENGE

Check your Job Spa goals for scope creep.

Time

Seeded throughout the previous weeks have been prompts to help you think about how your network has evolved since you started your job. As part of your Job Spa regimen, you have begun to evaluate, fortify, and expand your connections. Staying with the momentum of your Job Spa necessitates an occasional deeper dive into how you are managing time to support your networking. Take a deep breath. It's time to jump into the time-management pool.

First Things First

Continuing the thread of project alignment, let's see if the people you need to meet with have changed as a result of any milestone or project modifications. Any new colleagues need to be on your radar? Any changes in priority on your "need to make human contact with" list? Adjusting your network contact plans does not have to be a big deal. It takes a little effort to identify who these people are and when you need to contact them. To help transform this task from "I know I have to do this" to "Check that box":

- Block out fifteen minutes.
- Create a list of the people you need to contact.
- Next to each name identify the level of priority, how soon you need to contact them, and what information needs to be exchanged.

Within moments, that great glob of networking activities has been consolidated into a much more civilized list of the two telephone calls to make sure coworkers have all the information they need from you for their projects, the five e-mails with information you promised, the two documents you need to review and provide feedback on, and the five meeting invitations you need to send. Most of this can be completed within a half hour, if that! Phew.

Time to Do Lunch

Whether you meet someone in the company cafeteria, the sandwich shop next door, or at a nicer restaurant with a server waiting in the wings, food is a great way to connect. Lunch meetings are also less intense than conference room or office meetings. In a more social setting, the dynamics change. Your coworkers become less like corporate drones discussing the finer aspects of your next team-meeting agenda and more like normal people. Adding food to the mix can relax the mood. Plus, you have the ability to look away from your colleagues and turn your attention for just a moment to the art of the napkin fold.

Lunch meetings are a winning combination of fulfilling nutritional requirements and building work relationships. No time for lunch? Coffee break! It's away from your office or cube, food is readily available, and no one is suffering from the moody symptoms of low blood-sugar levels. Note: At the risk of damaging your image and shrinking your network, adhere to the tenets of good manners: proper use of utensils, chewing with mouth closed to avoid launching food bits, and elbows off the table. See *Miss Manners' Guide to Excruciatingly Correct Behavior* for further eating etiquette.

For those of you who telecommute, consider making a standing date in your calendar for an in-person lunch with different coworkers every couple of weeks and, if feasible, once per week. If you are remote, make it a point to go to the office once a quarter. As convenient as telecommuting is, do not get lulled into thinking that e-mail and phone can replace the impact of in-person contact.

JOB SPA BONUS CHALLENGE

Reach out to three people in your network with whom you have had no contact for at least a month.

Knowledge

Some parts of your Job Spa treatment require nothing more than kicking back and soaking it all in. Other times your Spa regimen requires a little exercise and breaking a sweat. Keeping with this week's theme of momentum, wade into the knowledge pool and do some sharing exercises. As you swim some laps and stretch your knowledge-sharing muscles, take an extra lap to think through the impact of what you share.

Do Something, Anything

Last week, it was great to think about the potential of all the things you can learn and share. However, your 100 Percent Commitment requires action. Think through the following questions:

- What new knowledge or information will I share this week as a part of my 100 Percent Commitment?
- How will I ensure that this knowledge is valuable to my teammates and coworkers?
- What new or additional knowledge will I take the steps to get this week as part of my reconfirmed 100 Percent Commitment?

Let's say, you decide to contribute your skills as an accountant. First, make sure that the skills you want to contribute are actually needed. As much as you revel in the joy of tax law, your peers in the design department may have no use for or interest in your accrual techniques.

After careful consideration and realization of your environment, the needs of the people around you, and your commitment, you realize that perhaps the glory of EBITA tax rules is not the best way to strengthen the "give" side of your commitment. Instead, you think about your projects, the needs of your teammates and coworkers, and identify a second love and interest that will impact your friends in design: design software. Bravo!

Deepening your inquiry to the next level, you realize that although you have dabbled with a few design programs, there is one program on which you want to become an expert. Based on the technology your company uses and the projects of your teammates, you conclude that this program will help tremendously. You also realize that the next best step is to learn more about the program and then share your skills and expertise with your team. Congratulations. You have achieved knowledge-sharing harmony!

JOB SPA BONUS CHALLENGE

Identify two new items you will share this week with coworkers.

Team

Your team and colleagues are a bit like your family. In every family, it is important to keep the lines of communication open and relationships smooth. As part of Job Spa progress, ensure things with your team are healthy and on track. Turn your attention to review your relationships. What relationships need to take priority? With whom do you need to make more of an effort? Reinforce your relationships. As part of strengthening your relationships and role-modeling your 100 Percent Commitment, consider where there are opportunities to coach your teammates. Yes, you can be a coach, and we'll get to that in a few paragraphs.

Review Your Relationship with Your Team

Over the course of time, the excitement and enthusiasm of your team's camaraderie may have lost its shiny glow. Don't let the love go. Remember the time when Dave crashed and burned during his presentation to the big VP of Sales and Ron saved the day? Or that time at the company picnic when Paula's quick thinking and skills with a lawn gnome kept Laura from Accounting from landing a combination of partially digested fajitas and too many margaritas in your lap?

Those were good times. Well, it's time to lay the foundation for more good times by looking at how you can strengthen team relationships.

Although your overall goal is to have strong working relationships with all your coworkers, what are the critical relationships that warrant attention? The degree of interdependency you have with specific individuals will determine how much attention you need to put toward strengthening those relationships. Your attention may also need to focus on patching things up with those individuals who challenge your inner Gandhi.

Once you begin to prioritize your relationships, dip beneath the surface and take a closer look at some of the dynamics. Here are some questions to gauge how well you are bonding. As you answer the questions, think about the team and any "special" individuals:

- Are your teammates/coworkers courteous and respectful in your interactions?
- When you asked them for help, feedback, and information, were they willing to help?
- How much do you know about your colleagues? Have you neglected to learn about them as people?
- What actions can you take to build stronger relationships?
- What actions can you take to strengthen how you are perceived as a team member or coworker?
- What actions can you take to role-model team behavior?

Reach Out

You have taken a closer look at the social experiment called coworker dynamics and how you are relating with others. Let's develop a clear plan for where and how to strengthen those bonds and manifest your commitment to *give*. Even if your relationships are already good, this is a great opportunity to make sure you continue to keep them strong.

Start your plan by identifying the people with whom you need to create better relationships. Start by taking care of any lingering items. Was there something that happened with crabby Robby that never got settled? Such as the time you forgot about your meeting and never apologized? In order to walk hand-in-hand off into the sunset, you need to resolve any lasting concerns.

Now that you have addressed any historical issues, focus on the future and how to avoid problems. Instead of complaining to the other person about his behavior or continuing to do something annoying to him, get clear on what can be done differently. Determine what specific actions you can take to make the relationship better. What requests do you need to make of your teammates that would create a more productive relationship? What new behaviors are *you* willing to commit to?

These ideas and plans you are developing to make your relationships stronger are all dandy, but they are of no benefit until you do something about them. Pick an appropriate time and place to have "the conversation." Make sure the conversation takes place in an appropriate and not-too-public location. Ask your coworker to meet you for lunch or make the time to go over to her cubicle or office and ask if she has a minute to chat as there has been something on your mind that you'd like to talk about. If necessary, find a conference room where you can talk privately. If it needs to be a longer conversation, schedule a meeting with enough time to talk through your concerns.

We hope you are now on course to strengthening and continually building great relationships with all your coworkers. As much as we want everyone to soak together in the Job Spa coworker hot tub of camaraderie, we realize this is not always realistic. It is natural that there may be a few folks who rub you the wrong way or whom you rub the wrong way. It doesn't mean that you avoid them. Take the initiative to establish a peace treaty. Understand their issues or concerns and seek a shared solution. Continue to take the higher road of professional behavior if your "special" colleague continues to thwart your peacekeeping mission.

Start Coaching

Once considered only in the realm of the sports world, coaching has now infiltrated almost every profession. In the context of your Job Spa, no skill area comes as close to embodying the essence of being a team player as coaching. Simply defined, a coach teaches and directs another person or group through encouragement, advice, and asking insightful questions. You probably never realized it, but you too are a coach.

You may already be intentionally or unintentionally coaching others during your conversations. Whether coaching is a recognized professional skill or common practice in your company, you will want to be a coach and have effective coaching skills.

Whether you are new to or experienced, here are some coaching guidelines to keep in mind:

1. *Permission:* Ask permission to offer your insight or assistance. You want people to be ready to hear your insights. Some people will ask you explicitly for your help while others will not. You do not want to overstep your boundaries with peers. If you identify an opportunity where you can help, first inquire if they would like help.
2. *Questions:* No matter your relationship with the individual, always phrase your thoughts in the form of a question. This gives the other person the option to take your advice. In some instances, because you asked a question, your coworker will be able to come up with

his own answers. When people make their own discoveries, they are more apt to accept this realization and commit to take action. The difference between giving advice in the form of a statement: "You should dress in a suit if you want to change your image" and a question "What are some things you can do to make your image look more professional?" is very important. The power of effective coaching lies in helping *others* identify and take ownership for new information or changes they identify.

3. Options for how to phrase your questions:
   - *Make it open ended:* "What are some ways you could get additional expertise for your report?"
   - *Offer your opinion in the form of a question:* "Have you considered going to Finance to get their help?"
   - *If the person asks for your advice, offer your opinion, and then ask him for his:* "You should take the report and run the numbers by someone in Finance because they would know better. What do you think?"
4. *Clear destination:* It is important that your conversation leads somewhere. Whether it is identification of a new idea, where to find a missing resource, or a shift in someone's attitude, effective coaching leads to a result. Whatever the person walks away with, make sure she walks away with something she can hold onto, think about, or more important, do differently.
5. *Commitment:* Get a commitment from the other person to follow up with you, or you commit to follow up with him. In even the briefest coaching conversation, establish a date or time in which you will reconnect. It's a good relationship-building skill to see how things went after your conversation. Following up also demonstrates that you care about the person and outcome. Last, you increase the likelihood the other person will follow through.

Effective coaching focuses on performance and tangible results, and usually tries to change behavior. One of the greatest challenges to traditional coaching is time. The pace of the work environment is constant and unyielding. Coaching is often thought of as a formal procedure that requires an in-depth conversation. In actuality, there are always opportunities to coach.

Effective coaching can take as little as a few minutes. Coaching is a function you perform by using a set of skills and can be applied in many interactions. You become a stronger team player when you demonstrate your coaching skills by helping others solve their problems.

JOB SPA BONUS CHALLENGE

Reach out to the person with whom you have the most challenging work relationship.

Image

Way, way back in Week Five, you spent time identifying, crafting, and practicing your personal PR plan and message. You've had some time to practice delivering your message. Let's see how your PR is being received and take it to the next level. Look in the mirror to ensure that your PR plan is fine-tuned and supporting your 100 Percent Commitment.

Your Amazing PR Message

Personal PR mastery takes time. Crafting the perfect message comes from honing your words and practicing your delivery. In the early stages of developing and delivering your message at the Image Salon, we didn't have you worry too much about getting the wording of your message 100 percent correct. The important thing was to clarify what you wanted to be known for and get in the habit of articulating your message. Now that you're sharing your message, in what ways have you noticed that the message could be tightened? Here are some tips to help you massage your message:

CHECK YOUR ATTITUDE. Your message must be supported by your verbal and nonverbal communication and behavior. If your message is one of creating relationships but your attitude is aggressive, you might want to chill out and convey a more relaxed demeanor.

REFINE YOUR KEY WORDS AND PHRASES. Revisit the specific words that support what you want to be known for. Are they still accurate?

BELIEVE IN YOUR OWN MESSAGE. Do you believe in your PR plan and deliver it with confidence? People will listen to you when you believe in what you are saying.

REFINE YOUR TIMING. Look again at your audience and the timing of your message. As you recall, you only need to deliver your message a few times on the right occasion for your words to stick. Remember, delivering your PR plan is not just about repetition and frequency. Think quality and strategic placement as well.

CONTINUE TO SHARE THE MESSAGE. It will get easier and more natural.

Ponder Your Interactions

How your coworkers perceive you began the moment they laid eyes on you. As part of your Job Spa, you are taking control of your image and ensuring that how others perceive you aligns with how you want to be perceived.

You are establishing an image strategy and implementation plan. Some of your changes may have been substantial; others have been slight modifications and polishing of an already well-oiled machine. You have developed your image based upon your new sense of the work environment, 100 Percent Commitment, and further insight into how you want others to see you. Think about your interactions over the last six weeks. Here are some questions to start your reflection process:

- In what ways am I using/practicing my PR message?
- In what ways are my coworkers responding to my message?
- Does my PR plan support my 100 Percent Commitment?
- Have I received feedback regarding my image? If so, are there any changes I should make and what should I continue to do?
- What words, actions, or components of my PR plan encourage people to respond?

Adjust your PR plan based upon your answers and discoveries. Reflect, revise, and test new behaviors and key words to see what resonates with your coworkers. Most important, have fun with your PR plan and message. This is your chance to experiment, test out new communication techniques, and gauge the reactions of your colleagues.

There's This *Thing* You Do

Do I really have potentially distracting habits? Of course you do. We all do. Don't pretend you don't know what they are.

Whether it is picking your face, rubbing your neck, talking too loud, habitually yawning, bouncing your leg, or tapping your fingers, each of us has an annoying habit that can distract others from hearing our desired personal PR message. Imagine your peer's loss of attention when you try sharing your message of detail orientation while simultaneously tapping out a tune with your shoe.

There have been plenty of people who have complained over the years about the annoying habits you have, whether they were parental figures, your significant other, a friend, or a previous coworker. If you cannot come up with anything, have the courage to ask a trusted friend or colleague. Don't let those little things drive folks away and undermine or distract from your PR plan.

Nonverbal and Verbal Signals

Keeping your image skills on track requires ongoing communication skill workouts. Don't overlook your nonverbal communication including appearance, body language, and tone of voice. Over the past six weeks, you have had a chance to reconsider your environment and how to make the most of it. This requires making sure that you are set up for maximum success. Don't let something you perceive as unimportant undermine your image. Is your cologne driving people away? Or did you forget to shower after your workout? You don't want an invisible force field that repels both people and insects.

Make sure your body language is open and inviting. Closed body language is evidenced by not standing up to greet people, continuing to read your e-mail when they come into your office or cube, and sitting with your arms crossed and brows furrowed. Open body language is inviting and pleasant for others to be around. Greet people with a warm smile and even a handshake, if appropriate. Sit in meetings leaning into the conversation and have a pleasant look on your face that tells people you are easy to approach and engaged. There's nothing worse than talking to a blank face. Don't make it as difficult for others as a Martian space probe looking for signs of life.

Your tone of voice makes a huge impression. If you sound annoyed, angry, or sarcastic, your teammates won't enjoy working with you. Not surprisingly, your coworkers want to have conversations that are lively and engaging. Make sure your tone of voice reflects your openness to engage others. Understand your audience before breaking out the jokes or sarcasm. Don't assume that everyone will understand your conversational ice-breaking humor.

People come back to experiences that are pleasant. How can you make the experience for others more pleasant when they are interacting with you? How can you use your verbal and nonverbal communication more effectively to build relationships?

JOB SPA BONUS CHALLENGE

Identify and practice two nonverbal communication behaviors that can help reinforce your verbal communication.

Put It All Together

Congratulations on completing the seventh week of your Job Spa. Before you get into the sauna to relieve the stress of the week, let's ensure you put everything into practice.

This week you are taking further action to strengthen your 100 Percent Commitment, look for opportunities to do lunch, coach your teammates, and hone your PR Plan.

Here is your calendar for the week. Plug in what you need to do in Week Seven to get your reflections and ideas into action.

Before you get ready for a well-deserved weekend, think back on the week. What went well? What did you learn? What do you want to work on or accomplish next week?

Congratulations on completing your seventh Job Spa week!

JOB SPA TREAT *for the* WEEK

Dress up your cube with something new that has your favorite color: a picture, a toy, or a lamp.

Calendar for Week (7) Day (1) 2 3 4 5

Time	Action	Notes
6:00 A.M.		
7:00 A.M.		
8:00 A.M.		
9:00 A.M.		
10:00 A.M.		
11:00 A.M.		
12:00 P.M.		
1:00 P.M.		
2:00 P.M.		
3:00 P.M.		
4:00 P.M.		
5:00 P.M.		
6:00 P.M.		
7:00 P.M.		

REMINDERS

- Be consistent: Match your verbal and nonverbal communication with your PR plan.
- Do lunch.
- Coach your teammates.
- Ensure your projects are on track (scope, milestones, and resources).

Calendar for Week (7) Day 1 (2) 3 4 5

Time	Action	Notes
6:00 A.M.		
7:00 A.M.		
8:00 A.M.		
9:00 A.M.		
10:00 A.M.		
11:00 A.M.		
12:00 P.M.		
1:00 P.M.		
2:00 P.M.		
3:00 P.M.		
4:00 P.M.		
5:00 P.M.		
6:00 P.M.		
7:00 P.M.		

Calendar for Week (7) Day 1 2 (3) 4 5

Time	Action	Notes
6:00 A.M.		
7:00 A.M.		
8:00 A.M.		
9:00 A.M.		
10:00 A.M.		
11:00 A.M.		
12:00 P.M.		
1:00 P.M.		
2:00 P.M.		
3:00 P.M.		
4:00 P.M.		
5:00 P.M.		
6:00 P.M.		
7:00 P.M.		

Calendar for Week (7) Day 1 2 3 (4) 5

Time	Action	Notes
6:00 A.M.		
7:00 A.M.		
8:00 A.M.		
9:00 A.M.		
10:00 A.M.		
11:00 A.M.		
12:00 P.M.		
1:00 P.M.		
2:00 P.M.		
3:00 P.M.		
4:00 P.M.		
5:00 P.M.		
6:00 P.M.		
7:00 P.M.		

Calendar for Week 7 Day 1 2 3 4 5

Time	*Action*	*Notes*
6:00 A.M.		
7:00 A.M.		
8:00 A.M.		
9:00 A.M.		
10:00 A.M.		
11:00 A.M.		
12:00 P.M.		
1:00 P.M.		
2:00 P.M.		
3:00 P.M.		
4:00 P.M.		
5:00 P.M.		
6:00 P.M.		
7:00 P.M.		

week eight
CHECK YOUR COORDINATES

"Last week was good. Before Job Spa it was so easy to spend my days simply working without having a bigger picture of what I want to achieve. Today, I am clear on what I am contributing and what I am taking in return for my contribution. Fine-tuning my PR plan has helped me clearly communicate what I value and my direction. I feel like I am on the right track.

"Things are moving pretty quickly. It's a good time to check in with my manager to let her know how I am progressing. This is also a good time to meet with some trusted coworkers to confirm if how I think I am doing is in sync with their perspective."

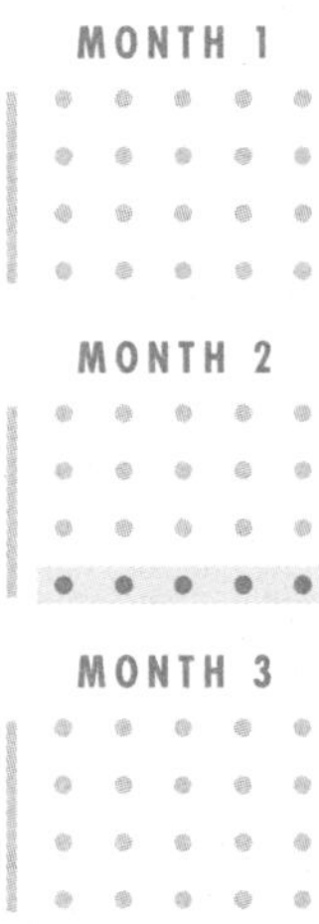

Welcome to Week Eight!

You have been working hard over the past two months to redefine what you want from your work and the ways in which you can make the best contribution to your company and coworkers.

In this week, catch your breath and make a pit stop at the water cooler to review your progress. As you rehydrate, take a look around. Check your pulse to make sure you are keeping stride and staying up-to-date on the latest trends that impact you. Review your priorities to focus your time and effort on the work that matters most.

WEEK 8	JOB SPA REGIMEN: TAKE A LOOK AROUND
GOALS	Review your progress.
TIME	Prioritize your work.
KNOWLEDGE	Scan your environment.
TEAM	Get a second opinion.
IMAGE	Practice your communication skills.

Goal

You are well on your way to Job Spa success. Like any spa treatment there is always room for an additional rub, scrub, or technique to improve your health. In your eighth week, take a look around to see how things are going and identify how you can strengthen your 100 Percent Commitment. What else do you need to do? What else can you do better? Check in with yourself and be honest. How are you *really* doing? The easiest way to gauge how you are progressing is to look at how well you are accomplishing your objectives.

On Track or out to Lunch?

When you started your Job Spa, you identified opportunities within and beyond the context of your current projects where you could contribute your ideas and develop your skills. You established objectives that support your 100 Percent Commitment. Now take some time to think about your progress and what you have accomplished. Deeper awareness of your progress and accomplishments will reinforce your 100 Percent Commitment. Even if you think that your 100 Percent Commitment is looking like your 75 Percent Commitment, we bet you've done a few things that have made a difference, and you should be proud of them.

Let's start with your Job Spa goals. What were they? Were your goals focused on developing your skills and qualifications, or expanding your knowledge to make yourself more marketable? Or were your goals to increase job responsibility, find a new career direction, or get a raise? Maybe your focus was to make the most of your current role and responsibilities. Take a few moments to confirm the progress of your Job Spa goals. Include that special goal you set for yourself as part of your analysis.

Here's another way to further dissect your goals. Goals usually fall into one of two categories: achievement and development. Each type of goal is interrelated; each is equally important.

Achievement goals are all about taking care of business and getting results. These goals set your sights on a specific destination. Development goals are what you need to learn to reach your achievement goals.

For example, your achievement goal is to become an electrical engineer recognized for at least five innovative patents and inventions. Great! What skills will you need to *develop* in order to become an electrical engineer who holds five patents? The development goals you identify—such as taking classes, getting your degree, and finding a top-notch mentor—will support your achievement goal to hold those five patents as an engineer.

Use the achievement versus developmental goal distinctions to understand the interrelationships existing between your goals and see if they need to be further refined to clear the path to your Job Spa goals.

Staying Power

In the work environment, there are many distractions and competing demands. As you review your progress and Job Spa objectives, how have you done? Are you on your way to accomplishing what you set out to do two months ago? Are your Job Spa goals realistic? If needed, alter them slightly to make the most of your work experience. Are there any additional skills you want to develop? You may also find that the skills you initially thought would be important are not so critical.

Revisit your trajectory by reviewing the following points:

- My Job Spa goals still reflect my 100 Percent Commitment.
- I know what resources I need to achieve my goals.

- I regularly update my plan to help me achieve my goals.
- I will reach each of the milestones I've set for my goals.
- I am clear what success looks like when I achieve my goals.

JOB SPA BONUS CHALLENGE

Identify which of your Job Spa goals are development goals and which are achievement goals.

Time

In conjunction with this week's theme of reviewing progress, consider how your time-management skills are supporting your success. This week focus on how you are prioritizing your work and making sure that you are maximizing the limited amount of time available.

Separating "Must Have" from "Nice to Have"

It can be tempting as part of your Job Spa to overextend yourself and aggressively set goals, to attempt to deliver great results on current projects, and to balance a handful of new, exciting objectives. Take a look at what is on your plate and make sure that you are allocating the right amount of time to the right things. We don't want to burst your bubble—just to catch your breath. Your first step is to take an inventory of what you are doing. *List* all of your projects, new skills/knowledge you want to develop, new projects you want to start, and put them into one of four categories:

1. *Mission Critical (important and time sensitive).* Identify the projects/work that are part of your job and are linked to how you will be reviewed by your manager. These are your mission-critical projects and need to be your number-one priority.
2. *Complementary Objectives (important and less time sensitive).* Identify the additional complementary objectives that link to your mission-critical projects. These may include training, research, and objectives that will help you go beyond the initial scope of your projects.
3. *Bonus Objectives (less important and less time sensitive).* Identify the objectives that fall outside your mission-critical or complementary objectives. This might include new goals, skills, classes, and aspirations.
4. *Time-Wasters (less important and not time sensitive).* Identify additional work-related activities on which you seem to spend your time. These activities might include side projects, surfing the Net, or extended chats with coworkers (beyond networking).

Review your inventory. Circle the areas in which you are spending most of your time. Are you spending your time in the critical areas: mission-critical and complementary objectives? Prioritize and deliver your mission-critical objectives on time and to the expectations of your manager and coworkers. Look at how the complementary objectives are progressing. These "extras" are important to look at because they will help bolster your Give 100 percent behaviors.

Your bonus objectives also need to stay on your radar. These objectives, although not a red-hot priority, can have great significance to your future. For instance, maybe you want to be CEO, which requires going back to school and getting an MBA. If you want to achieve your bonus objectives, you may have to spend nights, early mornings, and weekends working or studying. Among the many amazing things that your Job Spa has revealed is the potential of something beyond your current projects and role. Things have changed over the past two months. You have moved beyond fermenting in squashed aspirations to a place of new hope.

JOB SPA BONUS CHALLENGE

Expel one time-waster from your day.

Knowledge

When you started your Job Spa and developed your goals, you were prompted to take a strategic look at your industry and trends. This week, raise the periscope again to ensure the trends you took into consideration still make sense. Look at two areas: emerging trends and influences, and current best practices.

What's Hot Today *and* Tomorrow

As you have soaked in your Job Spa, you have probably done a bit of pondering and research before you fused yourself to your goals. The last thing you want is to set your sights in one direction only to find that your company has decided to move in the opposite direction. While there will always be unexpected or unforeseeable changes, increase your likelihood of success by staying on top of your research.

Start with expanding your initial search to include more sources of information. Do a thorough scan of the broader environment to discover industry best practices, trends, and potential influences. This can include recently announced acquisitions, market-share fluctuations, and emerging products and technologies.

Use resources outside your company. Talk to colleagues in other firms. Ask people if they are doing similar projects or observing similar trends. Your network can be extremely useful in this process.

Now take a look at your profession. What are the trends you are noticing two to five years down the road? For example, is there a continual move toward increased automation, outsourcing, or consolidation? What are the implications?

Finally, bring your quest closer to home: your company. You've already shopped your ideas around with your team and manager. If politically appropriate, tap any connections you have with any senior people. It can be amazing what's visible from just a level or two above. Find out if similar ideas or initiatives have been attempted in the past and what lessons were learned from those projects. What made them successful or not? Avoid redundant efforts, and more important, avoid projects that have crashed and burned. The last thing you want to invest your time and energy into is a phoenix without wings.

On a final note, make things easier on yourself by aligning your efforts with the direction of the industry, profession, and company. You can still be a maverick and introduce fresh ideas or a breakthrough perspective. Just provide context for how your objectives are aligned with the current direction and momentum of your environment.

JOB SPA BONUS CHALLENGE

Identify one new thing that's happened in your industry in the last month and its impact on you.

Team

Stay on track to build your team skills. Dust off the feedback skills you practiced way back in your first week. The good news is that information you gather this week is a bit more informal, and you may not need to go as deep as you did last time. Your main objective is to ensure that you are on track to realize your 100 Percent Commitment.

Feedback Again?

It's time to quench your curiosity with a drink from a tall, cool glass of reality. That's right . . . feedback time. Not to worry. You're a pro at this. This time it's going to be even easier because you paved the way two months ago, and you have been honing these skills ever since. Find your copiously written notes from when you first gathered feedback from your manager and coworkers. You did save your notes, didn't you? If you still have your notes, great! Dig through the data. If you tossed them, take a few moments to think about what you heard. What were your strengths, and what areas were identified as opportunities? What have you done over the past two months to strengthen your skills and improve how you are perceived? Now that you've reviewed your data and your memory banks, go back to get updates.

First, check in with your manager. Go straight to the top and ask how she thinks you are doing. Be sure to cover two specific areas:

1. *Work/project/role performance.* What is working well? Are there any areas that may need more attention? Gather any additional advice or guidance. Managers always like to feel involved and enjoy handing down pearls of wisdom.
2. *Your attitude.* As you know your 100 Percent Commitment shows up in your attitude. Ask about how your behavior is being perceived. This can be a little trickier than asking for input on your projects. Here are some sample questions: "Hi, (insert manager's name). In addition to getting your insight on how you think I am doing on my

projects, I also want to get your feedback on how you perceive my attitude and specifically my willingness to help others and make a contribution (insert other verbs that coincide with your PR plan). How would you describe my attitude? Is there anything else I can do to ensure I continue to support the team? On the flip side, are you finding that I'm clearly articulating what I need?"

Keep in mind that this meeting should be relatively informal. If your manager knows that you are taking a Job Spa, she will probably be aware of why you are asking her for this information. If she does not know that you are taking a Job Spa, let her know you've decided it's important to check in with her periodically to make sure that you are on the right path. State your intent only once. You don't want to come across as worried, paranoid, or overly concerned. Be calm, cool, and collected.

After checking in with your manager, it's time to cozy up to some coworkers to get their insight on how they think you are progressing. Ideally, you want to tap the people who provided your initial data. Probe gently because you don't want to sound as if you are fishing for compliments or lack confidence.

As a reminder, use the proper feedback protocol:

1. *Set the stage.* Ask for input regarding a specific event or behavior. For example, "Bruce, how am I doing regarding meeting our project deadlines? Are there any improvements or changes that I could make to be more effective?"
2. *Be specific.* Do not argue with the other person's interpretation. Instead, ask for specific examples of behaviors you displayed, other's reactions, and recommendations for what you can do differently. For example, "I really appreciate your feedback, Bruce. I want to make sure that I understand the specific things that I can improve. Will you give me an example of how I could have done a better job of setting expectations for completing my work?"
3. *Say thank-you.* Thank people for sharing their observations. As you know, giving feedback is not easy for others.

Remember, when you gather feedback, do not ask coworkers if they think you are giving and taking 100 percent. They will not know what you are talking about. Ask for feedback that coincides with your interactions and projects. Make them questions your trusted coworkers can answer with some certitude.

JOB SPA BONUS CHALLENGE

Get feedback from your manager this week.

Image

Your Job Spa is about increasing your level of professional fulfillment and is a conduit for new goals, perspectives, and getting more. Over the previous weeks we've explored what you want from your company, what you can contribute, and how to bring 100 Percent Commitment to life. The most important choice you have made as part of your Job Spa is to take action. Your image skills embody this decision. As part of the eighth week, ensure your PR plan incorporates actions that vaporize the workplace myths.

Burst the Bubble

The most important piece of making sure you are taking action and manifesting your 100 Percent Commitment is popping the balloon of the workplace myths. Remember?

▶ MYTH 1 **My boss/manager is my mommy or daddy and will take care of me.** *If you have a great manager, use him as a guide and resource. Also make sure that if he vanished tomorrow, you could still make it through the corporate jungle on your own. If your manager is the Grim Reaper, master the next steps in your own career, and have an escape route. Your PR plan can be an important mechanism in your escape. Which leaders know about you? What is your reputation in the company? These are all critical concerns when it comes to moving on.*

▶ MYTH 2 **My hard work will always be recognized and rewarded.** *Identify what you have been doing over the past seven weeks to communicate your projects, skills, and achievements. Yes, this stuff needs to be built into your PR plan and seeded into your everyday interactions. This is not about bragging about how incredible you are. This is about making sure that your skills and strengths are known and used. You should not wait to be asked, "What have you done to deserve another year of employment with us?" What you have done and what you bring to the table should be crystal clear to your manager and peers at all times.*

▶ MYTH 3 **Company loyalty equals job security.** *If you haven't picked up on this yet, please take this one kernel of advice: When it comes to your career trajectory, even if your plans are to stay with your current company, have plans A, B, and C. What are you doing to ensure that your skills are transferable to other jobs? Your PR plan needs to be aligned to support your career options. Do your coworkers (and people outside your company) know your strengths and talents? You want them to think of you when they come across opportunities.*

Skills to Help Burst the Bubble

You've worked hard to dispel these three myths over the past seven weeks. Continue to take action by shifting how you develop and use your communication skills. Your PR plan is dynamic and should continue to evolve as you hone your skills, practice new behaviors, and achieve new objectives. Let's take a quick look at how you've been building those PR skills. Start by looking at your communication techniques:

- Listening skills
- Asking and informing techniques
- Making clear requests

Are you really listening to what others are saying? When a message is conveyed, are you paying attention and looking for opportunities? Or are your thoughts going directly to what you want to have for lunch? Your ability to listen to others, to integrate the information, and to reflect back their major points is key to making sure you are hearing the messages around you. If you're not listening, how will you know you've burst the bubble? As a refresher, the keys to effective listening are stay quiet, do not interrupt, look in the general direction of the person talking, stay on topic, use key words, and paraphrase.

How are your "asking" and "informing" skills? To link back to the earlier skill, if you're not listening, your follow-up questions will not make sense. How are you asking effective follow-up questions? How comfortable are you with stating your opinion and advocating for your ideas? How adept have you been at informing your boss of all your accomplishments in the past two months? Remember the key to effectively asking and informing: to balance articulating your opinion with being able to invite others to contribute to the conversation.

Finally, let's move on to your request-making skills. How adept are you at asking for what you need? Maybe you've asked for too much over the years, and this has been your opportunity to scale back. Or do you still feel shy or think that perhaps you don't deserve something? If you don't ask for something, you decrease the likelihood you'll get it. Your request-making skill is crucial to making sure you ask for what you need in order to dispel those three myths. Remember the key points: Be clear on whom, what, and when.

JOB SPA BONUS CHALLENGE

In your next meeting, do all three communication activities: listen, ask and inform, and make a clear request.

Put It All Together

Congratulations on completing the eighth week of your Job Spa. Before you jump back into your spa regimen, let's ensure you put everything into practice. This week you've taken a step back to ensure you are on track. You've revisited your Job Spa goals to make sure they still make sense and will still be relevant when you've completed them. You have made sure they are prioritized, incorporated your teammates' feedback, and practiced your communication skills.

Here is your calendar for the week. Plug in what you need to do in Week Eight to get your reflections and ideas into action.

Before you get ready for a well-deserved weekend, think back on the week. What went well? What did you learn? What do you want to work on or accomplish next week?

JOB SPA TREAT *for the* WEEK

Get tickets to an entertainment event you enjoy (e.g., movie, concert, sport, play, or opera).

Calendar for Week (8) Day (1) 2 3 4 5

Time	*Action*	*Notes*
6:00 A.M.		
7:00 A.M.		
8:00 A.M.		
9:00 A.M.		
10:00 A.M.		
11:00 A.M.		
12:00 P.M.		
1:00 P.M.		
2:00 P.M.		
3:00 P.M.		
4:00 P.M.		
5:00 P.M.		
6:00 P.M.		
7:00 P.M.		

REMINDERS

- Step back and re-evaluate your Job Spa goals.
- Effectively prioritize your goals and tasks.
- Get feedback from your team about how you've done in the past two months.
- Practice your communication skills.

Calendar for Week (8) Day 1 (2) 3 4 5

Time	Action	Notes
6:00 A.M.		
7:00 A.M.		
8:00 A.M.		
9:00 A.M.		
10:00 A.M.		
11:00 A.M.		
12:00 P.M.		
1:00 P.M.		
2:00 P.M.		
3:00 P.M.		
4:00 P.M.		
5:00 P.M.		
6:00 P.M.		
7:00 P.M.		

Calendar for Week (8) Day 1 2 (3) 4 5

Time	*Action*	*Notes*
6:00 A.M.		
7:00 A.M.		
8:00 A.M.		
9:00 A.M.		
10:00 A.M.		
11:00 A.M.		
12:00 P.M.		
1:00 P.M.		
2:00 P.M.		
3:00 P.M.		
4:00 P.M.		
5:00 P.M.		
6:00 P.M.		
7:00 P.M.		

Calendar for Week 8 Day 1 2 3 4 5

Time	Action	Notes
6:00 A.M.		
7:00 A.M.		
8:00 A.M.		
9:00 A.M.		
10:00 A.M.		
11:00 A.M.		
12:00 P.M.		
1:00 P.M.		
2:00 P.M.		
3:00 P.M.		
4:00 P.M.		
5:00 P.M.		
6:00 P.M.		
7:00 P.M.		

Calendar for Week (8) Day 1 2 3 4 (5)

Time	Action	Notes
6:00 A.M.		
7:00 A.M.		
8:00 A.M.		
9:00 A.M.		
10:00 A.M.		
11:00 A.M.		
12:00 P.M.		
1:00 P.M.		
2:00 P.M.		
3:00 P.M.		
4:00 P.M.		
5:00 P.M.		
6:00 P.M.		
7:00 P.M.		

week nine
ADJUST YOUR TRAJECTORY

MONTH 1

MONTH 2

MONTH 3

"Last week I met with my manager to provide an update on my projects. This meeting went really well. I requested her feedback on my projects, and she told me that she is pleased with my work. I asked her some specific questions about how I am performing and if she had any recommendations for improvement. Luckily, there were no surprises. The only suggestion for improvement was continuing to manage how much I commit to, so I don't overpromise and deliver late. Overcommitting was never an issue before Job Spa!

"Last week I also met with a few trusted team members who gave me some feedback that will help me move forward. It was good to get confirmation that they are seeing a difference in my attitude. They say I seem to have more energy and focus."

Welcome to Week Nine!

In this week of your Job Spa, you put into action your discoveries from last week. Find your Inner Work Guide. This ensures you are operating at peak performance. As you make progress during your invigorating ninth week, you will have the opportunity to refresh how and what you are sharing with your coworkers, and continue to stay on point with your collaboration and coaching. Last, you will finish this week's spa session with a visit to your Image Salon.

WEEK 9	JOB SPA REGIMEN: REVISE AND READJUST
GOALS	Reflect, recenter, and refocus.
TIME	Adjust your time-management skills.
KNOWLEDGE	Adjust what and how you are sharing.
TEAM	Adjust how you are collaborating and coaching.
IMAGE	Adjust your personal PR skills.

Goal

No Job Spa would be complete without the opportunity to continue to balance your worker chi, burp your inner corporate child, or pat the belly of your subconscious CEO Buddha. Before you incorporate what you learned last week, stop, take a breath, and consider the principles of who you are in the context of what you do.

Your Inner Guide

Warning: The following paragraphs may contain language and examples not suitable for those who get squeamish, nauseated, or scared when dealing with potentially squishy topics such as feelings, emotions, meditation, and introspection. However, included in this section are some familiar statistics. Reading and working through this next section will help you broaden your experience and perspective for how you experience your job and help strengthen your 100 Percent Commitment.

This week, your goal is to meditate on your experience of work. What work represents to you, how it fulfills you, what you need to increase fulfillment, and your awareness of who you are both as a unique individual and employee. This week you'll consider the meaning that work brings to you or what it *can* bring to you.

Work is a critical part of who we are as human beings. We have a psychological need to "do" and "feel" a sense of accomplishment and identity through our efforts. Although what we do varies from trash collector to artist to salesperson to astronaut, the human experience of self and work is very much the same. Isn't it interesting that according to a 2004 Gallup poll more than 70 percent of people are disengaged from their job, but over 70 percent of individuals would continue working even if they didn't need the money? How do you interpret this? What does this mean for you?

Over the past eight weeks, you have set off on a new course to address this disconnect and create alignment between what you do and who you are. You clarified the value of your contribution and what you get in return. Your 100 Percent Commitment sums up this conscious shift.

Continuing down this path, do a bit of introspection and discovery. Even if you are a member of the 30 percent who would take the money and run as far from work as possible, the following section will help you find greater satisfaction until the big payday comes your way.

Workplace Enlightenment

In what ways does your work provide you with a sense of fulfillment? Even if you are a hard-core pessimist and loathe your work, company, and work environment, there must have been at least one event, project, or occasion where you felt good about something you did at your job. What kinds of activities or interactions give you this sense of accomplishment? What can you do to increase these kinds of opportunities, interactions, and/or events?

Second, increase your awareness in your daily activities. Focus on one thing at a time. Try moving from multitasking to single tasking. When you draft an e-mail, focus on that activity. Consider the intent of your message, the words you are using, how the reader will feel or what he will know once he reads it. When you talk with a customer or coworker over the phone, focus on your conversation and only that. What is your customer really asking for? What is your coworker really requesting of you? Be present in every single moment of your activities.

This may sound counterintuitive, especially in our world of multitasking. Experiment with single tasking for the week, and at the end see if you are less stressed and more focused. When you focus on one activity, do you find that you are more effective and make fewer errors? Do you find that your mind is calm, you listen better, and you are more mentally engaged?

Third, understand the context of your work and its place in your larger career trajectory. A substantial part of your Job Spa has centered on helping you define the context of your current work and new objectives and begin to consider your larger career path. Define the links between the tasks you perform today, your job and its responsibilities, and the bigger picture. Today's activities may seem menial at times and a waste of your potential. Reframe this perspective. Even the most mundane task is part of your larger trajectory. It must be given as much attention and value as the tasks that you perceive as critical.

Fourth, recognize and appreciate yourself as an individual and as an employee, and for your unique contribution. Throughout your Job Spa, we have explored defining what you know, your perspective, and how to contribute that perspective given the culture and dynamics of your company. Take this very seriously. In light of company politics, team, and individual dynamics, it can be easy to lose sight of who you are and what is important to you. Consider the following questions:

- What knowledge, skills, and perspectives make me unique?
- What is the best way to maintain my sense of self and contribute my strengths to my company?
- On the job, when I'm not focused, bringing forth my best, and living my 100 Percent Commitment, what's going on for me?
- In what ways can I address this lack of alignment?

Fifth, think about your immediate work environment: your office, cube, or desk. Identify what you can do to create an environment that helps you focus, find calm when you need to catch your breath, spark creativity, or bring a smile. Consider adding colors that can soothe your psyche in one area and others that will energize you. Don't create a dumping ground for junk on your desk. Consider adding a small toy or puzzle that can distract and amuse you when brain fatigue sets in. Décor makes a difference.

Hang in there . . . we are just about done with the soft, squishy stuff. We hope you took at least one of these recommendations to heart. Thinking through these points and increasing your awareness of who you are and what you do gives you the ability to understand the benefits you derive from your work.

Time

Over the previous eight weeks, you placed greater demands on yourself and increased your workload. There are probably times when your to-do list is about to explode. Since you've been Job Spa training in the past two months, you are in peak condition to achieve Job Spa actualization, which requires a balance of strategic introspection with achieving the tactical demands of the workday. As you venture through this week of introspection and action, it's time to take a look at how your time-management skills and practices are holding up.

Taming the Beast

As you incorporate the ideas of becoming more present and aware at work, think about how you choose to plan, track, and allocate your time. Although your routine may be the antithesis of spontaneity and excitement, it is also the bedrock of your ability to manage a most precious resource: your time. Let's take a moment to review and appreciate what having a routine can do for you. Your routine provides you with the opportunity to manage your schedule because you know where your schedule can be adjusted and where things must stand firm. Your organized routine supports you for the unexpected. With your routine in top condition, you are prepared to take on any new planning challenges. It's time to review, revise, and reinstate your routine.

Take a quick inventory to help you review and revise your routines to ensure that they still fit your needs.

- Do you arrive early or on time? When do you want to arrive? What would be most helpful given how much you need to accomplish during the day?
- Do you get all of your daily goals accomplished? Do you set realistic expectations or do you try to squeeze too many things in a day and set yourself up for disappointment? What will you adjust?
- Do you make it to meetings on time? What will you adjust to make sure you are showing up on time?
- Do you leave work at a reasonable hour? What will you adjust to leave at a reasonable hour?

The purpose of having routines is to enable you to have a structure in place that helps you to be your best. Manage your time effectively to provide a measure of predictability.

Underpromise and Overdeliver

By now you know that successful, on-time delivery of your projects takes more than luck—it takes planning. Planning is critical unless you are an adrenaline junkie who thrives on the rush of a suddenly remembered deadline. As you continue your time adjustment, review how you are delivering your projects.

First, review your project scopes and deadlines. Are they reasonable given the time frame you've allocated? Remember the golden rule: It is better to underpromise and overdeliver than to overpromise and come up short! This can be incredibly embarrassing and more important, can undermine your 100 Percent Commitment. Job Spa is here to help you get rid of this ugly habit. Make your project scopes and timelines realistic. Lower your level of anxiety and make people happy to see your amazing work . . . submitted early!

Next, take a look at how well you are creating a time line in which to achieve your goals. Incorporate your insights from last week about the mission-critical objectives, complementary objectives, bonus objectives, and time-wasters. What changes do you need to make to your existing project time lines and milestones so that you are set up for success? Finally, incorporate your changes from last week into your calendar and your two task lists (general task and daily task lists).

Make the choice to underpromise and overdeliver. Like exercising and eating right, time-management stuff is relatively dry and not the sexiest of subjects, but it is also one of the most important areas to master. When you actually take these little steps seriously, you will see a transformation in how you work. In addition, as you become adept at managing your time, you will find that your level of stress drops and that familiar feeling of overload can be put back in its place because you know how to organize and plan. Don't just think about it, do it.

JOB SPA BONUS CHALLENGE

Complete everything on this week's daily task list.

Knowledge

It's great when you can pick up the phone, send an e-mail, or walk down the hall and get the information you need. That's a healthy network! Your Job Spa has helped you take a closer look at your relationships, at how information is shared, and at solidifying the information and knowledge you have to share. Last week you looked at trends in the industry and profession. This week, let's take a look at what and how you've been sharing. What more can you do?

Give It Up

Giving is not just for the holidays, birthdays, or germs. First off, are you sharing? Come on now. Fess up. You have been busy over the past few weeks, and it's possible that sharing has not been the first thing on your mind. Good going if you have been sharing consistently with your coworkers and reaching out and expanding your network by volunteering relevant information. If your sharing has been a bit on the lighter side, it's time to rethink and revive the caring-and-sharing gene. Let's get back in the groove and share with the people around you.

We hope that your coworkers have noticed your new, improved level of commitment and have been supportive. Continue building goodwill. Reciprocate if they have been reaching out to you first. Sharing should be as automatic as your habit of chewing gum with your mouth open or hanging up on telemarketers at the first sign of a pitch. However, if your psyche has not yet internalized the sharing behavior, be proactive. Set a weekly sharing objective. Make the choice to identify one thing per week to share with specific individuals or a group (i.e., your team, department, or cross-functional team).

Make It Count

Now that we have prompted you to share again, let's switch gears to look at *what* you are sharing. Even if you reviewed the previous section and smiled confidently that yes, you are sharing, make sure it has value. Shocking as it may sound, not everyone wants to know about every blind date you've been on this past month.

Sharing simply to check that activity box is a risky activity for the Job Spa devotee who is truly committed to her success. Danger lies ahead if your recipients find little value in what you are sharing. Your information and you will eventually become a nuisance. This can erode the image you are working so hard to build and reinforce. Make sure that you have reviewed the needs of your audience before announcing your next knowledge jewel that everyone must have. Err on the side of caution, and take into consideration your targeted audience. Don't use the catch-all commercial drift-net approach.

Finally, give context to your sharing. Explain why you are sharing your information with your audience and the logic behind your intent. A little context can go a long way to ensure that others perceive your actions as sincere as opposed to brownnosing.

Go for a Home Run

Last on the list, take a closer look at *how* you are sharing with your intended audience. Remember the three important aspects of how to share: audience, information, and result.

What does your audience need to know? Do they need high-level information or do they want the details? Are they going to read the report that you are sending them, or will it take a presentation and discussion for them to digest and use the information? The audience is asking, "What's in it for me (WIFM)?" They don't really care about "what's in it for you." This sounds a little cold, but it's true for the most part.

What's the WIFM for your audience? What are they going to get out of your hard work and effort? What are they going to get for investing their time to hear your update? Make it worth their while. Tailor your message to your audience. Most people think they do this, and do it well. Think again. How can you ensure you don't fall victim to this illusion?

What is the most effective way to present information? Is your audience composed of visual learners? Do they like graphs, charts, and pretty pictures? Or are they auditory learners who just need to hear the information once? Are they kinesthetic learners who need to talk and play with the idea to understand it? Maybe you decide your audience has all those needs and figure out a way to show them the information, engaging them in a lively discussion and using the white board to get them to draw the connections. Adjust the way you deliver information for maximum impact.

What do you want from sharing? Do you want someone to read your information as an FYI? Do you want a stamp of approval? Do you want someone to find a way to incorporate it into his project? Do you want to generate a conversation about possible solutions? Be clear on your intent. What do you want people to do with the information? So next time you e-mail Joe another link to a video clip of a bulldog riding a skateboard, think about what you want. Yes, these videos are quite funny, but if all you are sending is that kind of information, try again. "Hey Joe, hope you enjoyed that skateboarding video. Thought you would like it, given your love for dogs and skateboarding. I also wanted to let you know about a great article I came across in today's finance section about our competition. I thought it might provide a different angle for the product you are marketing."

Your call to action is clear: Read the article, and see if it gives you another angle to beat the competition. Get clear on the results you want and let the other person know.

JOB SPA BONUS CHALLENGE

Determine if your manager likes information delivered visually, aurally, or kinesthetically.

Team

Keeping to the theme of making adjustments for maximum effectiveness, we turn our attention to the topic of your team player skills. As part of your 100 Percent Commitment and achieving your Job Spa goals, make the choice to collaborate and look for opportunities to coach your teammates and coworkers. That's right—it's caring and sharing time! Again!

Collaboration Exfoliation

The weeks are racing by, and that's why it is crucial that you continue to keep looking for opportunities to collaborate. You need to exfoliate those layers to reveal the glowing team player. Let's take a moment to get real.

- Are you meeting the expectations of your team and coworkers?
- Are you living up to your 100 Percent Commitment as it pertains to your teammates and colleagues?

Whether you answered a confident living-in-reality yes, a tentative "maybe," an "I swear I'm going to change my ways," or a flat-out no, it's time recharge your team player batteries.

At the start of your Job Spa, you went through a challenging process of understanding what you want from your job and what you want to give back: your 100 Percent Commitment. As part of realizing this commitment, you decided to give collaboration an even harder push. You scrubbed down the layers of the shell that have built up over the years and found your baby skin still intact. You reached out, even to your archnemesis, Peggy, and paved the way to a new relationship.

Looking forward, what do you need to adjust or continue to do to keep sloughing off all those dead cells that can so quickly accumulate and leave you dry and crusty? Take a look at your projects and the projects of others around you. Who else and what other departments can you bring into the fold of your continuing mission of collaboration?

We're not asking you to keep going back for more punches from Peggy if things have not gone as smoothly as you hoped. As long as you've done your part to reach out authentically (not because you want to check that box) on several occasions for a particular topic/project, then you're okay. You've tried and can point to having tried. You even have the bruises to prove it. However, you're not quite off the hook yet. You can still do your part to keep the peace and ensure you are professional at all times. Your 100 Percent Commitment means that no one in your workplace can accuse you of not being a team player. You always reach out, are ready to help, and always act as a professional.

A Refreshing Coaching Drink

In Week Seven we talked about the concept of coaching and how to coach your coworkers. Although Week Seven feels like yesterday, keep coaching on your radar screen.

Flashback: Coaching is taking the initiative to help others. You may not have the answers to their problems, but you are willing to listen. There are times people want to vent for the sake of venting. Be there for them. This may open up coaching opportunities.

How do you know the difference between venting and wanting a solution? That's an easy one . . . simply ask. You don't have to be a mind reader. Gently say, "You sound pretty frustrated. Do you think it's just the way it is or is there a possible solution?" You may get one of two responses, "Yeah, I'm just so frustrated that this is just the way it is. Thanks for listening." Or the person could come back with, "Yeah, I'm really frustrated. This keeps happening not just to me, but to others as well. I need to do something about it."

People will let you know where they want to take the conversation. Your role as a coach is to help them get there quicker. Either you'll listen and the other person will feel better, or you'll keep asking him questions about what solutions have been attempted and what solutions are possible. He may even surprise you and come back with a new idea on his own! That's the beauty of coaching.

Take a look at the past few weeks. Did you attempt to coach? Did you help someone talk through a solution? Moving forward, what would it take to remember to see if you can lend a helping hand?

JOB SPA BONUS CHALLENGE

Have two coaching conversations this week.

Image

It's Job Spa image-tweaking time! Over the past few weeks, you have reviewed and refined your 100 Percent Commitment and your goals. Make the choice to communicate your 100 Percent Commitment by having your image and PR plan aligned. Remember, the intent of your PR message is to communicate your *values* and what you want to be known for to a broader audience. Review and update your image as part of an ongoing process. Let's look at how you can adjust what and how you communicate.

Lather, Rinse, Repeat

Adjusting your image to support where you want to be is like staying on track with a fitness regimen: Identify a realistic program, do your cardio, tone those muscles, try new exercises, and incorporate the program into your life for sustainability. For Job Spa sustainability, review your PR plan to ensure it's working for you and that you are consistently "working out." Communicating your image should be fun. Test out a new behavior, add some words to your PR message, and even consider expanding your repertoire to a new audience. This visit to your Image Salon is a great chance to try something new on for size and test it. Lather, rinse, and repeat.

Adjust Your Thermostat

Take a close look at your current PR message and continue to refine it. The intent of your PR message is to communicate your *values* and what you want to be known for to a broader audience. Your PR message should not nag or whine about what you think you deserve. Your PR message should be used not only to advertise what you want.

Separate your values and what you want to be known for from your goals. For example, if your goal is to work on a highly visible project within six months, then communicate in your PR message your values around hard work and accountability. You want others to know through repetition and delivering a consistent message that you value accountability. When you communicate this value, it makes you an attractive candidate for the project because people know what to expect from you. Conversely, only repeating that you want to be a part of the project sounds as if you are nagging and fails to provide others with an understanding of what you can contribute. Thus, regularly repeat your PR message to a broad audience, and only once or twice communicate your goals to key individuals.

Here's another example. If your Job Spa goal is to increase your skills to make sure you get on a high-visibility project, your PR message should be about what you value: to continuously grow your skills to add value to your projects. So you might say, "My projects are going well. Thank you for asking. I'm enjoying them because I can apply my skills from last month's training. I'm really looking forward to continuing to grow my skills in the upcoming months."

Review the message and delivery of your PR plan. Ensure you communicate why you would be a valuable asset to a project team. It's different than requesting or whining that you want to be on a project. If you need to articulate your goals and make clear requests for what you want, then do it once or twice at the appropriate time and place and to the key people who have influence (i.e., your manager or project leader). Keep your PR plan separate.

JOB SPA BONUS CHALLENGE

Separate your PR message from your goals.

Put It All Together

Congratulations on completing the ninth week of your Job Spa. Let's inventory what you need to do as you smooth out all the wrinkles this week.

You've started this week by recentering on work and your job. You want to find meaning in your work. You've found opportunities in your workplace to help coworkers by collaborating and coaching and to help yourself by refining your professional image and PR plan.

Here is your calendar for the week. Plug in what you need to do in Week Nine to get your reflections and ideas into action.

Before you get ready for a well-deserved weekend, think back on the week. What went well? What did you learn? What do you want to work on or accomplish next week?

Congratulations on completing your ninth Job Spa week!

JOB SPA TREAT *for the* WEEK

Celebrate Monday! Plan something special for a Monday evening (i.e., go out to dinner or cook your favorite meal).

Calendar for Week (9) Day (1) 2 3 4 5

Time	Action	Notes
6:00 A.M.		
7:00 A.M.		
8:00 A.M.		
9:00 A.M.		
10:00 A.M.		
11:00 A.M.		
12:00 P.M.		
1:00 P.M.		
2:00 P.M.		
3:00 P.M.		
4:00 P.M.		
5:00 P.M.		
6:00 P.M.		
7:00 P.M.		

REMINDERS

- Find your Inner Work Guide.
- Find opportunities to collaborate and coach your coworkers.
- Hone your image and PR plan.

Calendar for Week (9) Day 1 (2) 3 4 5

Time	Action	Notes
6:00 A.M.		
7:00 A.M.		
8:00 A.M.		
9:00 A.M.		
10:00 A.M.		
11:00 A.M.		
12:00 P.M.		
1:00 P.M.		
2:00 P.M.		
3:00 P.M.		
4:00 P.M.		
5:00 P.M.		
6:00 P.M.		
7:00 P.M.		

Calendar for Week (9) Day 1 2 (3) 4 5

Time	Action	Notes
6:00 A.M.		
7:00 A.M.		
8:00 A.M.		
9:00 A.M.		
10:00 A.M.		
11:00 A.M.		
12:00 P.M.		
1:00 P.M.		
2:00 P.M.		
3:00 P.M.		
4:00 P.M.		
5:00 P.M.		
6:00 P.M.		
7:00 P.M.		

Calendar for Week (9) Day 1 2 3 (4) 5

Time	Action	Notes
6:00 A.M.		
7:00 A.M.		
8:00 A.M.		
9:00 A.M.		
10:00 A.M.		
11:00 A.M.		
12:00 P.M.		
1:00 P.M.		
2:00 P.M.		
3:00 P.M.		
4:00 P.M.		
5:00 P.M.		
6:00 P.M.		
7:00 P.M.		

Calendar for Week (9) Day 1 2 3 4 (5)

Time	*Action*	*Notes*
6:00 A.M.		
7:00 A.M.		
8:00 A.M.		
9:00 A.M.		
10:00 A.M.		
11:00 A.M.		
12:00 P.M.		
1:00 P.M.		
2:00 P.M.		
3:00 P.M.		
4:00 P.M.		
5:00 P.M.		
6:00 P.M.		
7:00 P.M.		

week ten
THRIVE IN REALITY

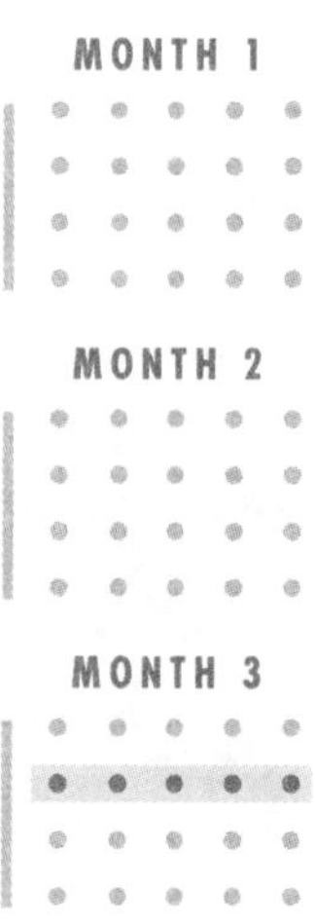

"I guess you can always be surprised. I thought I knew my company really well. I made a presentation last week outlining recommended changes to the customer-intake process to a group of VPs. I thought I had my information well prepared, my presentation was detailed, and laid out perfectly . . . I was in the zone. But wow! After about ten minutes, one of the VPs asked me a question about the expected results of my project in comparison to our major competitor, who has made similar changes. Luckily I had an answer that was well received. What really surprised me was that they wanted recommendations and results, not just an overview of the project, history, and big picture. The presentation agenda was shared and confirmed by the audience prior to the meeting. I walked into the meeting with the assumption that I was making a high-level overview presentation of my work.

"Although I made it through this experience in one piece, it definitely made me think about the real work environment. What are the unspoken protocols for projects and what people really expect? On the surface I can see certain obvious things about my company's culture. This week I am going to look more closely at what's beneath the surface and not just take things for granted as simply the way things are done."

Welcome to Week Ten!

As part of your Job Spa, you've soaked, scrubbed, stretched, and sprinted your way to career health. You are a few weeks away from graduation. For a dose of preventive maintenance to ensure you continue to stay healthy and happy, take a look at the real work environment around you. This will help you navigate the terrain and maintain momentum for your 100 Percent Commitment.

In previous weeks, you started evaluating certain elements of your work environment. Now that you've had some time to implement Job Spa goals and skills, let's see how the environment has reacted. When you understand the real work environment, you are better able to stick to your 100 Percent Commitment, navigate obstacles, and focus your resources.

WEEK 10	JOB SPA REGIMEN: DEFINE THE REAL WORK ENVIRONMENT
GOALS	Define the real work environment.
TIME	Define how time is really used, pace, and how deadlines are set.
KNOWLEDGE	Define how information is really shared.
TEAM	Define how people really work together.
IMAGE	Define the real image of success.

Goal

During your first weeks on the job, it was tough to figure out just how anyone got anything done. The realization and understanding of your company's "uniqueness" comes with time and experience. Your understanding is especially put to the test when you try something different . . . like applying your 100 Percent Commitment.

Your goal for this tenth week is to reflect and incorporate your observations of your experience within your company. This clearer picture of your workplace will help you better prepare for the future and sustain your 100 Percent Commitment. To decipher your environment, stop to think about how work gets done, how relationships are valued, how politics play out, and what it takes to really succeed.

Playing by Their Rules

Every company has its own set of rules, processes, and behaviors. These unique elements reflect the culture of your company. Some are visible, easy to point out, and logical in how they support the successes and effectiveness of the company. Other behaviors, processes, and rules that are part of the company culture are less obvious and sometimes invisible until you stumble upon them during your work or when you stretch yourself to be 100 percent committed. Whether the rules are smart or stupid, it is important to stay open and flexible to your environment. This week is an opportunity to confirm and leverage your understanding of the company culture.

Clarifying the *C* Word

So what is company culture and how do you identify it? Management professor and organization culture guru Edgar Schein suggests that to better define and understand organization culture, you should look at it as having three levels:

LEVEL 1 *Artifacts.* They are generally visible and readily identifiable. In your company, artifacts might include the structures, work processes, and the awards you see on the walls.
LEVEL 2 *Values.* A company's espoused values include its goals, strategies, and philosophies.
LEVEL 3 *Underlying assumptions.* A company's basic underlying assumptions include its beliefs, which are often taken for granted.

For example, you walk into a company and marvel at the onsite gourmet cafeterias and striking artwork. What a nice environment!

These visible artifacts (Level 1) are physical manifestations of the espoused values of the company (Level 2): "to make the work environment comfortable for our employees." The underlying assumption (Level 3) is that a comfortable employee is a happy employee, and a happy employee is more likely to be productive (because he is eating on location and not out running personal errands), stay with the company long-term, and attract talented new hires.

How does organizational culture form and evolve? It begins with the creation of the company. The founders either intentionally or unintentionally infuse their values into their company. The kernel of a company's culture may blossom from a variety of sources: an initial set of rules, the founder's values, or underlying beliefs. In the years that follow, the manifestations of these values or assumptions evolve. Culture becomes a part of the company's DNA. When people try to change the culture abruptly, the system naturally fights back, treating the changes as a virus and attacking them.

As you re-examine your company's culture and the ways in which business operates, what do you notice? What values does your company espouse and how do these values translate into actions? Use Schein's model to focus and organize your observations:

LEVEL 1 *Artifacts.* These are easily seen, such as the look of the work environment, ways in which work gets done, or company practices. Look at both organizational structure and processes. Are there lots of layers of management or is it relatively flat with a few leaders? Does your company require tons of paperwork to get even the smallest things done? Does your company provide onsite child care and free drinks? What does the pizza and beer party every Friday afternoon say about the company's values around networking and having fun? Are operating rules and procedures visible? For example, some organizations have meeting guidelines posted in every conference room.

LEVEL 2 *Espoused Values.* This is what the company says about the way it conducts business, how employees treat each other, or how the company treats its employees. What does the mission statement say? Does your company clearly state its values? Are the values embedded in how the work gets done? Some organizations ensure their espoused values are visible to every employee by placing them on posters, Web site, and ID tags. Do employees and management embody these values or disregard them?

LEVEL 3 *Assumptions.* What do all the artifacts and espoused values mean about the basic assumptions the company has? What are the differences or similarities between the artifacts, espoused values, and the assumptions? For example, for Level 1, the company provides free drinks. Everyone loves that. For Level 2, the company says it values its employees. Level 3 (and your conclusion) is that employees are happier when they are hydrated. No, silly. It says that the company tries in small and big ways to take care of its employees' basic needs.

This is your opportunity to play detective. What are you noticing about your company culture? Are the levels consistent?

Cold Splash

As you begin to better define your company's culture, don't be surprised to find that your earlier perception of your company may have changed. That's okay. This can be a good thing. Understanding the components of your company's culture can help explain those things that aggravate you. They may continue to baffle you, but at least now you have some context for why they occur and what you can do to make the most of the culture.

Most company cultures comprise a combination of factors that are great and not-so-great. Just like people, companies are not perfect. One of the results of your exploration over the last nine weeks is honing your adaptability to take the good and effectively manage the bad. What do you appreciate about your company culture? What areas require blinders or a doctor's special attention? The parts that are not so ideal you can keep in an "improvement areas box" in your mind. You don't necessarily have to do anything about them, just be aware so that you are navigating your workplace with maximum agility.

Finally, compare your ability to navigate your company culture before and after you started Job Spa. How are you fitting into the culture? Are you leveraging what you know about the culture to be more effective? Master the various cultural elements of your company to continue to give and take 100 percent.

JOB SPA BONUS CHALLENGE

Identify one thing you do that reflects the company values.

Time

Over the past nine weeks, you have become more conscious of how you manage your time and have begun to practice skills that take the idea of time management from concept to behavior. Keeping with the theme of defining your real work environment, get a clearer picture of how time acts as an influence in your company.

The influence of time on your company comes from a range of sources including your company's industry and founders. To better decode how time is treated, think about it at three levels: company, department, and individuals on your team.

Your Company—Tortoise or Hare?

Each company will vary in how time influences pace, strategy, processes, and behaviors. One company may take forever to get a project off the ground while another company can quickly go from concept to execution.

As you look closer at the pace of your company, consider the following:

- Your company's industry
- The unique company methods and processes that can either expedite or slow the pace of work
- Your company's sense of urgency

The pace of your company's industry is a powerful influence. Many industries have calendars that dictate research and development cycles, production, and market launch. Whether it is the fashion industry that lives by the seasons or the accounting industry that is driven into frenzy each year around April, it's important to understand how the industry influences your company's pace.

In your company there may be institutionalized methods and processes for how decisions are made and work is done. These internal mechanisms can greatly influence the pace within your organization. Keep your eyes open for how decisions are made, what steps are involved in introducing a new idea, and how long it takes to get that new idea off the ground. If there is a lot of bureaucracy or decisions are made by consensus, ideas will take longer to implement. Consider the major methods and processes your company uses.

The pace of your company is also influenced by either a lack of or a heightened sense of urgency. This level of urgency can be part of your organization's culture: "Things are always crazy around here." Or it can be a response to an external threat such as a new competitor or an internal concern: "If we don't get that new paperweight to market on time, our numbers for this quarter are squashed." What is your company's sense of urgency? How does your company compare to the competition?

As part of your 100 Percent Commitment, what time behaviors do you need to adjust to be more effective in operating in your company's culture? Be strategic in your pacing, expectations, and the demands you place on others. Understand whether your company is a speedy type A or a cautious slower mover—and why. This will help you match the pace or even look for ways to tone things down or crank things up as needed.

Walk, Jog, or Run with Other Teams

As part of your Job Spa tutelage, you have expanded your line-of-sight and work horizons beyond the silo of your department and have begun the practice of networking and sharing with coworkers. As part of continually expanding your cross-organization perspective, compare the broader company to the pace of the various departments and teams with whom you interact. Don't be surprised if you find wide variations in how time is treated. While the company pace has some impact on the pace of a department or team, the major pacesetter (no pun intended) is the department or team leader. How much this individual drives for results and progress determines how fast the department or team moves.

As you look at your department and team, determine the following:

- What is the pace of my department? How does this compare to other departments?
- What is the pace of my team? How does this compare to other teams? Is the pace of my department or team on track, too fast, or too slow?
- What do my department and team need to do to keep pace with others around us?
- How does leadership influence the pace? Who is the "leadership?"

Identify opportunities to tune up time practices in your company, department, or team. Take a closer look at the specific elements that are perhaps causing things to be out of whack. Your research should be informal and probably stealthy. No point in causing paranoia among your teammates because you are looking to root out the causes of organizational inefficiency.

If you discover inefficient work practices or that the pace needs to be adjusted, think through potential solutions. Selectively share your new ideas. See how they are received. If others are receptive, volunteer to work on any related tasks. If you discover that it is not so much the work process as the workers, back up slowly and don't make any sudden moves. Demonstrate political acumen. It is probably not worth naming names unless you are directly impacted.

Team Fun

Your Job Spa plans more than likely involve, or to some degree depend on, teammates. Take a look at the pace of each person on your team. This will help you adjust your expectations, plan more effectively, and build better rapport. When it comes to each person on your team, there will likely be wide variations regarding how time is valued and each person's pace.

You are probably already aware of the range of your teammates' pace. Like Bikram yoga and spinning classes, the extremes are hard to forget. Some folks are super-speedy and intense, while others seem to exist in another dimension in which time moves just . . . a . . . little . . . bit . . . slower. Confirming the pace of the people on your team will help you know what to expect when you work with them. You won't need to set yourself up for an aneurism each time you talk to Curtis and Charlotte. You will know that Curtis requires a bit more time to get things done, and Charlotte talks so fast that you will need to take notes to make sure you get the details of her request. As an added benefit, knowing the pace of your teammates will help you be more effective in collaborating with and coaching them.

Take a moment to reflect on the following:

- How quickly do other people on the team get projects completed?
- How quickly do others on the team return e-mails and voice mails?

- What are the hours others on the team work during a typical day?
- How do you compare? What do you need to do to keep pace with them?

Let's take a moment to look at the larger time picture. As you take a closer look at the three levels of pacing in your company, take a step back to consider your actions over the previous nine weeks. Were your Job Spa goals supported or thwarted because of how time is treated? Now that you have a greater awareness of time, what modifications do you want to make moving forward with your Job Spa goals, current projects, and any future projects/ideas you have?

JOB SPA BONUS CHALLENGE

Change one thing about your own pace to be more in sync.

Knowledge

A big part of deciphering the hieroglyphics of your work environment is decoding the mechanisms and subtleties of how information is shared. It's time to play corporate anthropologist and investigate what you may have taken for granted. Job Spa success requires that you are dialed into the right sources of company, industry, and job-specific information. Although you have been on the job for some time, it is critical that you bring a fresh pair of eyes to see how you can effectively get the resources you need.

Fertile Soil of Knowledge

How freely is information shared in your company? As you reflect on your quest to gather information to support your Job Spa goals, how easy or challenging has information been to obtain?

- When you reached out to coworkers for input, who stepped up to share?
- What parts of the company, department, and team culture dictated what could be shared?
- When you needed additional information to do your job and pursue your Job Spa goals, how much effort did it take to find and secure the knowledge and information?
- When you asked for further skill development and training, were you supported?

Each company, department, and team has various ways in which information and resources are made available. What have you realized about how information and knowledge are shared? What priority is placed on employee development? What can you do to make gathering information and knowledge easier?

Gold Star for Sharing

As part of your Job Spa self-actualization, you've been prompted in the previous weeks to look at what knowledge and information you have to share with your teammates and others in your company.

How receptive have your coworkers been to your sharing your inner wisdom, new ideas, strategic insight, and knowledge? You've taken the initiative and at times taken a risk by stepping out of traditional company behaviors to share information and role-model new behaviors. How did the company, department, and team respond?

Has your knowledge sharing benefited others and been recognized by your coworkers? Or do you feel like a lone voice crying out in the woods? Your company is just not ready to hear you. If you are a lone voice, double-check that you are presenting the information in a way that others can hear. Remember the whole idea of speaking to your audience? Take into consideration the culture of your company. How can it listen and integrate your knowledge? WIFM: What's in it for me?

Master effective sharing practices so that you create opportunities in the future to share your ideas in a way that's digestible for others in your company.

JOB SPA BONUS CHALLENGE

Try one new method for sharing your information.

Team

One of the things we have emphasized is the importance of having a team player attitude. This attitude is a major component of the "give" piece of your 100 Percent Commitment. Ah yes, that team player ethos is a splendid thing! Over the past nine weeks, you have been honing your team player skills and building reserves in your karma bank account. As you continue to look at your real work environment, take a look at how your team and coworkers manifest team spirit. You will be in a better position to develop, deploy, and influence others when you have an even better sense of how others are willing to practice corporate "Kumbaya."

Don't Be the Piñata

Over the past nine weeks, you've had the opportunity to experience team dynamics in the context of your Job Spa. With this different perspective, assess whether your team is indeed a cohesive group of people dedicated to common goals that values group success as much as individual success. The importance of effectively collaborating and the benefits of strong relationships are universal. Be aware of how close your teammates are, what they value in terms of communication and follow-through, and how they demonstrate a commitment to each other. Assess your team against these standards:

- The team holds itself accountable.
- If one person fails, everyone fails.
- If one person falls, others are willing to lend a hand (coach).
- People are willing to work with each other (collaboration).
- The team delivers on what it says it will do.
- The goals are shared, clear, and measurable.

WE'RE NOT SAYING that you need to become the new piñata for your team's misplaced frustration. Look for subtle things that you can do to rise above the fray and lead others to the land of team effectiveness.

How does your team fare? Regardless if your team scores high or low, moving forward are you willing to lead by example? What can you do to be a dynamic leader of your team? Perhaps your team has joined the dark side and is fraught with dysfunction, politics, and positioning. What a great challenge and opportunity to look for ways to role-model and influence new behaviors.

You Do Trust Me, Right?

So here is a sticky subject: trust. Trust is defined by *Webster's Dictionary* as "a firm belief or confidence in the honesty, integrity, reliability, justice, etc. of another person or thing." Are you confident that if you needed help your team or coworkers would provide it? Do members interact honestly? Or do they hold back the truth? How much do you trust your team, manager, and coworkers?

Trust is the key to how well a team and company works together. If members do not feel as if they can trust one another, they are less likely to collaborate, communicate effectively, coach, and work to achieve shared goals. Based on your Job Spa experience, assess whether your coworkers have trust by observing how they communicate with each other, follow through on commitments, and assist each other.

How do you ascertain if there is trust and how do you get it back if it's been lost? Here are five behaviors that break down what comprises trust:

1. *Care.* Do your coworkers care about what happens to others? Do you?
2. *Candid.* Do your coworkers speak openly and honestly?
3. *Accepting.* Do your coworkers respect and accept differences in opinion and ways of being? Do people openly agree to disagree? Do you?
4. *Credible.* Do your coworkers know what they are talking about? Do you?
5. *Consistent.* Are your coworkers consistent and reliable? Do they regularly do what they say they will do? Do you?

We hope there is a strong level of trust among your coworkers. If the level of trust is lacking, consider what you can do to increase trust with each of the individuals to maintain a healthy glow and youthful appearance.

Job Spa has directed you to seek out and interact in ways you may not have done before. Your behavior has required you to take some risks and trust that the people around you will treat you fairly and be honest. You've had to balance the reality of the workplace (i.e., politics, ego, turf-guarding) and take on a sense of optimism to look at the potential your work environment holds. The risks you've taken have helped you to learn and grow.

You've Lost That Lovin' Feeling

Like any long-term relationship, things can go wrong. A simple misunderstanding can turn into a big deal that becomes a part of corporate lore. Remember when Laura drank the last diet cola in the fridge, thinking it was hers? This little event escalated into a universal corporate practice of labeling every single food item employees put in the fridge. And of course, the rumor started that she couldn't be trusted.

If you realize that some of the trust has been lost between you and your colleagues, you can do something about it. Yes, you can gain back trust, even if you did take that last diet cola. Since the five trust elements are based on behaviors, there are tangible things you can do. You can be more credible in what you say and do. You can be more consistent in your actions.

It takes willingness, time, and diligence to rebuild trust. How do your realizations about your coworkers and the level of trust impact your behaviors and expectations? Given your 100 Percent Commitment, what behavioral elements of trust do you need to practice or do you need from others?

JOB SPA BONUS CHALLENGE

Identify one coworker with whom you need to rebuild trust.

Image

A big part of your Job Spa experience is going to the Image Salon on a regular basis. Take a closer look at the mirror to determine not only how great you are but to make sure you are looking just as good to the folks around you. Over the past nine weeks, you have taken a serious look at yourself and made a few tweaks based on your discoveries. Test your assumptions to make sure that the mirror you have been staring at reflects the real work environment. Compare yourself against the image that is recognized and rewarded by the company. Look at the types of image and behaviors that stand out.

You Are a Walking Billboard

Last week we discussed how presenting your image can be a powerful and effective way to communicate and reinforce your PR message. You are a walking billboard. Are you overdue for a haircut, facial, or manicure? What you wear and your body language advertise who you are. Even if you are having a bad hair day, the show must go on. You are a professional at all times. You have had some time to think about the image you want to create and to begin to support that desired image through your dress and behavior. You have also had time to observe the image and profile of others and how they are perceived.

It's time to review whether people are treated differently based on the image they portray and ensure that your image is on track and supports what you want and how you want to be known. For example, does your company seem to reward people who dress professionally more than those who wear shorts and a T-shirt? Does management take certain individuals more seriously because they present themselves in a more conservative manner? What do you need to do to make sure you have the eyes and ears of the right people?

You may find that certain profiles get more attention from senior management than others. This is not a matter of right or wrong; it is simply a fact of business life. If you were a senior manager looking at the next generation of organization leaders, you would more likely notice someone who looked the part rather than someone who presented himself in a very casual manner. Right or wrong, people will judge you based on the image you convey.

Your Job Spa goal is to succeed in your work environment. It would be nice to change the company's culture and perception of what a company leader should look like, but is that where you want to expend your energy? That could be an uphill battle and a waste of your time. After you make CEO, you can institute a change in dress policy. In the meantime, focus your energy on tuning your image to reinforce your success. Based on your observations and feedback from previous weeks, what is the image of success in the company?

You may also notice that certain kinds of body language receive more attention than others. And no, we are not referring to sexual body language. It's more about body language that demonstrates enthusiasm for a project versus one that says you are feeling lukewarm and unenthusiastic. Your body language is a reflection of your internal attitude. If you walk around thinking the glass is half full, it will show up in your body language. You may have noticed that those who get excited about projects actually get considered for them. Go figure! Or those who show excitement about any outcome of their project, regardless if it's positive or negative (what they learned from the experience), actually are recognized for the work they did. What body language is recognized and rewarded in your company? How do you tweak your body language to get the recognition you desire?

It Talks, Too!

That's right. You not only look good, but you can also put together well-constructed sentences! Let's just make sure the noises you make are reinforcing what a superstar you are. Tuning your image to support your 100 Percent Commitment requires understanding the value your company and coworkers place on what people say. You may find that some people in your company are great talkers. Whether they produce much work, they receive positive attention from key members of management because they consistently and frequently present information on their work.

You scratch your head in disbelief that this person is considered a high performer? *You* are involved in more projects that are even *more* challenging. "What is going on?" you ask. This person is conveying a message that she is involved in a lot of busy, complex work. It is not so much that she is doing a lot of work, but the detailed way in which she communicates what she is doing creates the impression that she is very busy doing a lot of important things. As much as this nauseates you, use it as an opportunity to look at yourself. What do you need to do and say to get your message heard? While it's not in your nature to fluff up what you are working on, perhaps there's a more effective way to show your peacock feathers, too. Sometimes one sentence is not enough to convey all the great work you are doing, try two sentences (one update and one descriptor).

Beyond frequency and level of message detail is also the content in other people's messages that is recognized and rewarded. What words or phrases grab attention? What spoken values does the company seem to reward? What key words or phrases seem to get noticed? Some of these words are nothing more than jargon, but power words have true meaning and significance to your company. Incorporate these power words into your repertoire, and into your PR plan, in a way that's authentic.

Your keen discernment of the image skills that are rewarded in the company is an important exercise. Developing your image is an evolutionary process that will continue long past your twelfth week of Job Spa. Look for ways to hone your image and ensure it is supporting your needs. Have fun as you develop, change, and adapt. Crafting your image is a great way to try a new style, practice your communication skills, and demonstrate who you are and the value you contribute.

JOB SPA BONUS CHALLENGE

Identify the power words in your company, and then determine if they are jargon or if you want to incorporate them in your message.

Put It All Together

Congratulations on completing the tenth week of your Job Spa. Let's ensure that after you've dunked yourself into the reality pool, you rise to the surface and put everything into practice.

You've taken a closer look at your company, department, and team. You've faced the realities of your work environment. You are now operating from a more informed place. This has allowed you to adjust your expectations of your company and yourself, including pace, information-sharing, trust on your team, and the image of success.

Here is your calendar for the week. Plug in what you need to do in Week Ten to put your reflections and ideas into action.

Before you get ready for a well-deserved weekend, think back on the week. What went well? What did you learn? What do you want to work on or accomplish next week?

Congratulations on completing your tenth Job Spa week!

JOB SPA TREAT *for the* WEEK

Have your favorite food for lunch.

Calendar for Week (10) Day (1) 2 3 4 5

Time	Action	Notes
6:00 A.M.		
7:00 A.M.		
8:00 A.M.		
9:00 A.M.		
10:00 A.M.		
11:00 A.M.		
12:00 P.M.		
1:00 P.M.		
2:00 P.M.		
3:00 P.M.		
4:00 P.M.		
5:00 P.M.		
6:00 P.M.		
7:00 P.M.		

REMINDERS

- Exhibit trust-building behaviors.
- Be the image of success.
- Keep pace with your environment.
- Network to get timely information.

Calendar for Week (10) Day 1 (2) 3 4 5

Time	Action	Notes
6:00 A.M.		
7:00 A.M.		
8:00 A.M.		
9:00 A.M.		
10:00 A.M.		
11:00 A.M.		
12:00 P.M.		
1:00 P.M.		
2:00 P.M.		
3:00 P.M.		
4:00 P.M.		
5:00 P.M.		
6:00 P.M.		
7:00 P.M.		

Calendar for Week (10) Day 1 2 (3) 4 5

Time	Action	Notes
6:00 A.M.		
7:00 A.M.		
8:00 A.M.		
9:00 A.M.		
10:00 A.M.		
11:00 A.M.		
12:00 P.M.		
1:00 P.M.		
2:00 P.M.		
3:00 P.M.		
4:00 P.M.		
5:00 P.M.		
6:00 P.M.		
7:00 P.M.		

Calendar for Week (10) Day 1 2 3 (4) 5

Time	*Action*	*Notes*
6:00 A.M.		
7:00 A.M.		
8:00 A.M.		
9:00 A.M.		
10:00 A.M.		
11:00 A.M.		
12:00 P.M.		
1:00 P.M.		
2:00 P.M.		
3:00 P.M.		
4:00 P.M.		
5:00 P.M.		
6:00 P.M.		
7:00 P.M.		

Calendar for Week (10) Day 1 2 3 4 (5)

Time	Action	Notes
6:00 A.M.		
7:00 A.M.		
8:00 A.M.		
9:00 A.M.		
10:00 A.M.		
11:00 A.M.		
12:00 P.M.		
1:00 P.M.		
2:00 P.M.		
3:00 P.M.		
4:00 P.M.		
5:00 P.M.		
6:00 P.M.		
7:00 P.M.		

week eleven
DECLARE VICTORY

"Last week I walked the corporate hallways like a detective seeking clues as to the real work environment. What I realized was not surprising, but it was certainly a good reminder. People have been receptive to my Job Spa attitude and goals, but I can also see that some people are threatened and annoyed that I'm super-duper engaged. They just need to take a Job Spa themselves. I need to remember and incorporate what I learned last week into some actions.

"As I'm getting closer to the end of my Job Spa treatment, I want to maintain momentum. To keep up my 100 Percent Commitment, I will continue to make the skills and behaviors an integrated part of my work."

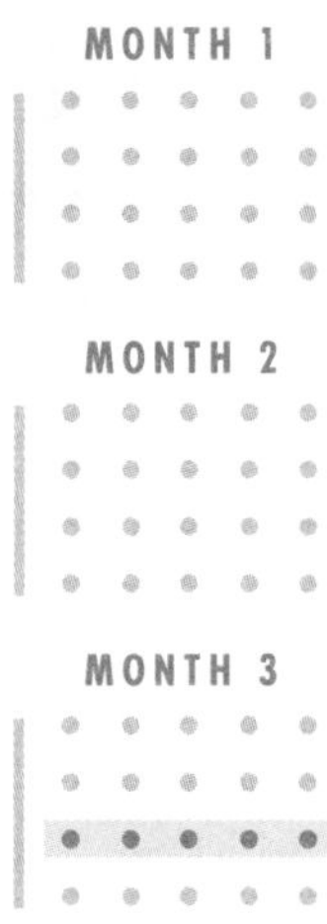

Welcome to Week Eleven!

You are getting close to the end of your Job Spa. Over the past ten weeks you have identified new goals, confirmed your 100 Percent Commitment, reinforced connections with coworkers, and are performing like a champion. Last week you took the plunge to look closer at the real work environment with a new perspective and eye toward what you can do differently to strengthen your 100 Percent Commitment. This week, dry off from your dip in the pool of reality. Focus on taking action on the observations you made in the previous week to hone and implement your Job Spa skills. This is your final Job Spa checkup.

WEEK 11	JOB SPA REGIMEN: ALIGN AND SUSTAIN YOUR SKILLS AND BEHAVIORS
GOALS	Execute your Job Spa strategy in line with the real work environment.
TIME	Apply your time-management skills in line with the real work environment.
KNOWLEDGE	Apply your knowledge-sharing skills in line with the real work environment.
TEAM	Apply your team skills in line with the real work environment.
IMAGE	Apply your image skills in line with the real work environment.

Goal

You spent last week reviewing the realities of your company and recalibrating your expectations of your environment and yourself. Build on this information to continue cultivating your balance and resiliency. Take a look at your goal-setting and implementation skills based on what you learned last week about your company's culture. As part of this effort, you will determine areas of improvement to ensure that the goals you set become a reality.

Formula for Success

This is an exciting time as you are approaching your third month of your Job Spa! As you review your technique and methods for achieving goal success, integrate your observations and *aha*s from last week's real work environment scan. Begin your review by comparing where you are today with when you began your Job Spa treatment. Aside from your desire to give and take 100 percent, what other factors are contributing to your success?

> **GOOD TIMING?** Do you find yourself in the right place at the right time? Do you do enough research to know that certain individuals are important to your project? When you see them, do you know the right questions to ask? How did you get the other person to divulge information? Is it more than just good timing?
> **GOOD PLANNING?** Absolutely! As you know, good planning makes a big difference. Know your success metrics (i.e., what you will see, hear, and feel) and milestones, and ask for resources. Do you give yourself enough time for each section of your project? How were you able to get the precious resources you needed?
> **GOOD EXECUTION?** Of course! Your ability to plan and then implement is key. This is the balance every employer is looking for. The skills you have and the questions you know to ask make your ability to deliver a lot easier and more effective.

You have the formula for success! Make any additional tweaks or changes to build resiliency and sustain you for the long haul.

Peak Performance

As you think about your achievements over the last two and a half months, how did you contribute to the team? This is not about how you were *as* a team player. This is about whether you met the goals and expectations of your team. In the early weeks of your Job Spa, you gathered feedback from trusted coworkers. You also identified how you could contribute to your team as effectively as possible. Did you meet, exceed, or fall short of the expectations that were set?

It's important to review your progress and accomplishments to determine what you did that worked and identify what you need to adjust. Think of this as fine-tuning. Like any amazing piece of machinery—whether a Steinway grand piano or a quad-carbureted

Ferrari—your goal skills can always benefit from some fine tuning to maximize your performance.

Take a look at your Job Spa goals. What additional fine-tuning do they need to optimize your success in the real work environment? Do you need to push harder? Or can you ride the momentum?

JOB SPA BONUS CHALLENGE

Identify one goal-setting skill you can tune up.

Time

Urgency, pacing, and patterns have taken on a whole new meaning since your immersion in Job Spa. Last week you took a close look at how your company, various departments, and individuals embody these very same concepts. It's time to build upon your observations from last week and adjust your time-management practices for continued success. Review your routine and your ability to prioritize and implement your projects in a timely manner.

Mastering the Daily Routine

As part of your Job Spa, you've gotten into the groove and flow of things at work. How has your daily routine supported your ability to manage time? Are you in and out of the office at a decent hour that meets the expectations of your coworkers and your family? Congratulations if you have your routines down to a science. If they can use a bit more refining, here are some reminders to help you:

- Leave your meetings on time to get to your next meeting.
- Plan to arrive at your meetings two minutes before they start.
- Get back to people on time. Let the other person know that day that you've received their request. And add it to your daily task list.
- Before you head home, clear your voice mails and e-mails at the end of every day.
- Align your internal clock with your external clock. (Do you think ten minutes has passed when in reality twenty minutes have gone by?)
- Stay devoted to using your calendar and task list.

The Art of No

Your Job Spa has helped you stay balanced by focusing on the most important priorities in your job and career trajectory. There are times you may take on tasks and projects that don't support your 100 Percent Commitment. Get clear on what those are. If needed, find a way to get them off your plate. Remember scope creep and those orphan projects? As you continue to focus on the most important things to you and your success, use the simple yet powerful word *no*. The importance of getting comfortable with saying no is twofold:

1. You confirm your boundaries.
2. You assert your priorities to others.

With just one syllable, you have saved time and distraction from what is important.

Drawing on last week's theme about your company's culture, how do others in your company successfully say no? You want to be able to refuse in such a way that you don't offend or upset others. Sometimes people do it so well that you don't even hear the word.

In fact, you feel as if you should thank them. Other times, rejection sounds like a two-year-old who's just learned to say no. What can you garner from your coworkers' artful techniques of saying no?

Caveat: We are all for on-the-job boundary setting. However, don't practice your "talk to the hand" skills in response to all requests.

Thirty Minutes or Less . . . Guaranteed

You can plan all you want, but if you do not execute the beautiful, elaborate plans you drew up, those plans are worthless. Worse, you undermine your image. Successful execution is about bringing your plans to life. Reflect on how you are executing your work. Given what you've learned about the pace of your company, department, and individuals, what will it take for you to pick up the pace? To deliver on the plans and promises you made, review your project plan and milestones so you are not giving yourself too much time. Rather, you are in sync with your environment.

Don't forget your favorite Job Spa tool—and we're not talking about the tanning lotion—the other one, your task list. Use it regularly to keep you focused. Your ability to deliver your high-quality projects in a timely manner is extremely important to your 100 Percent Commitment. Keep up the great work, and continue to put your plans into action!

JOB SPA BONUS CHALLENGE

Identify one task or project you need to take off your plate.

Knowledge

Over the past ten weeks, you have been feasting on as much information and knowledge as possible. Some of what you have gathered you have thrown back and some of what you have is good enough to sink your teeth into. In this week's Knowledge section, review your skills and consider ways to make sure you are on track to sharing your knowledge resources with the people around you.

Modern Hunter-Gatherer

Take a closer look at the knowledge and information you have gathered over the past two and a half months. How did you know what you needed and where did you get it? Take inventory of what you have learned over the past weeks and any other knowledge that you think would be valuable to others. Document your knowledge. Consider what you learned and how you found it. What about the culture of the company made this information easy or challenging to forage? It's amazing how much information you can acquire in ten weeks. It is your ability to obtain information that will keep you toned and fit. What works best for you?

Now that you know how to get food and bring it back to camp, how adept are you at sharing your sustenance? What exactly are you good at sharing and with whom? Given your revelations from last week about your work environment, what do you need to do differently to ensure that you continue to successfully gather and share information that supports your 100 Percent Commitment?

It's All about Whom and What You Know

Your network has played an important part in what you have learned and the skills you've acquired over the past two and a half months. By now you should have a growing network of coworkers and even people outside your company as sources of information. Over the past ten weeks, we have been your Job Spa consultants supporting you in getting information and knowledge from the people around you, *and* in sharing what you know. Before you can declare victory, identify your favorite ways to reinforce your network.

Gift Basket

Before you grab the phone and start calling your colleagues, reflect on your previous forays into the realm of sharing. Consider what has worked well and also consider what may not have been so effective. Consider these four simple rules:

1. *Know your audience.* Identify what specific information is relevant.
2. *Create a package.* Make the information as usable as possible. Make sure you put in the WIFM (what's in it for me).
3. *Deliver the package.* Identify the most effective way to share.
4. *Assess the value.* Follow up with your audience to confirm the value or benefit of what you shared and if any additional information would be helpful.

Your knowledge skills will support your 100 Percent Commitment today and for many years to come. Keep fine-tuning them.

JOB SPA BONUS CHALLENGE

Do two things this week to reinforce your network.

Team

Your team skills are all about collaboration and coaching. In retrospect, how proactive have you been in building relationships with your coworkers and ensuring that you make the best effort to be a team player? As you get closer to finishing your Job Spa, keep the momentum. Continue to collaborate and coach whenever the opportunities arise. Given your perspective on the real work environment, assess your team player skills and determine what you need to adjust to continue to coach and collaborate.

Together Forever

Collaboration skills are the heart of being a team player. You've been asked to do many sets and repetitions to exercise this muscle. How have you collaborated over the past ten weeks? Were you willing to work with others or compelled to stick to old habits?

From your detective work last week, you've noticed that your work environment may or may not be conducive to a strong team player atmosphere. This certainly impacts the degree to which you were able to demonstrate your collaboration skills.

Determine where opportunities to collaborate exist and where you need to proceed with caution. Certain coworkers might always want to work together whereas you might get a chunk taken out of your leg if you push someone else too much. Don't be discouraged if people didn't initially embrace your willingness to collaborate. Just use some savvy and know where and when to make an effort.

Review your collaboration skills and your efforts. Ask the following questions:

1. Did you step up every opportunity you got? Or did you avoid additional responsibilities for fear of taking on too much?
2. How does your work environment support collaboration?

3. When you offered assistance, did you find the experience personally gratifying? Did it strengthen your commitment to your work?
4. How did it contribute to strengthening your work relationship with the other person?

"Yeah, I am all about collaboration!" You may think so. However, the real test is whether others would describe you as collaborative. To confirm that you are indeed putting the *C* in collaboration, talk to a few coworkers to see if your perception matches theirs. Do you need to jump in and roll up your sleeves? Do you need to involve more people in your projects to make sure their needs are reflected in the end product? Do you need to demonstrate that you care about their opinions?

Your minor tweaks and increased reps of your collaboration muscles will give you a tremendous return on the time and energy you invested to support and sustain your 100 Percent Commitment.

Lend a Hand

Coaching muscles are a natural extension of your collaboration muscles. As you know, coaching is not about your willingness to help others with a few kind words of inspiration. Save the kind words for your mother-in-law.

As you thought through the real work environment last week, how have you been able to coach others on your team? In what ways have your coworkers been receptive or resistant? How do you need to demonstrate your coaching skills in a way that's consistent with the company culture?

Here are some great reminders and tips from Week Seven to help you make the ongoing effort to coach as the opportunities arise:

1. Offer your insight or assistance instead of providing unsolicited or uninvited input.

2. No matter your relationship with the individual, always phrase your thoughts as a question. Here are a few suggestions for how to phrase your questions:

- Make them open-ended: "What are some ways you could get additional expertise for your report?"
- Offer your opinions as questions: "Have you considered going to Finance for help?"
- If the person asks for your advice, offer your opinion, and then ask for hers: "Take the report and run the numbers by Finance because they would know better. What do you think?"

Based on your findings from last week and your current coaching skill set, how do you want to tone your muscles to ensure you stay 100 percent committed? Coaching is your gift to others.

JOB SPA BONUS CHALLENGE

Identify one person to coach this week.

Image

Your image skills have been critical to how you are perceived. Your look, attitude, and demeanor have evolved from "This is who I want to be" to "This is who I am." Before concluding that you are a PR genius, let's do a quick review to ensure that you are indeed all that you can be. Set your sights on what you've done well with respect to your communication skills, PR message, and network. Then determine areas that require finishing touches to make your professional image stick.

Communication Skills

Your verbal and nonverbal skills are the first things people notice when they interact with you. They convey your professional image. You've done a great job in the past two and a half months of making sure you are more aware than ever about how you portray yourself. Take a look at the communication skills and techniques. What finishing touches do you want to apply based on the real work environment?

- *Professional look:* What is your look? Do people see you and automatically think you dress the part? How are you making sure you stay groomed and well manicured? Don't let any of this slip. You've done a great job of portraying a professional image.
- *Body language:* Do people know when they see you that you are open and willing to help? How are you demonstrating through your body language that you are pleasant and energizing to be around? How are you sitting in meetings (i.e., leaning into a conversation vs. crossed arms and leaning back in your chair)? How are you using your face to convey a positive message (i.e., smiling and making eye contact vs. furrowed brows and looking away at the clouds)?
- *Active listening skills:* How is your ability to listen? Are you letting others finish their sentences? Are you repeating key words and paraphrasing what others have said to confirm that you are both listening and understanding their view?
- *Rapport building skills:* How are you building rapport with others? Are you making small talk and learning about others' professional

and personal lives? Are you matching their tone of voice, key words, and body language to be in sync and create comfort and trust?

- *Request skills:* How do you make requests of other people? Are your requests specific in terms of what you are asking and when you need it? Are your requests answered? Are you feeling shy or confident about making requests?
- *Asking and informing:* Do you ask questions to understand the other person's point of view? Are you able to effectively state your opinion on something? What about your ability to do both in a conversation to ensure good exchange of information?

Wow! That was a long list. Can you believe you've been working on all these communication skills and techniques for the past two and a half months? As you celebrate your accomplishments in building your communication skills, incorporate modifications that will support your undying 100 Percent Commitment!

PR Guru

Your PR message communicates to others who you are and what you stand for. You've done a great job of delivering your message with frequency and consistency. Now let's see how it's working to support your 100 Percent Commitment.

As you walk the halls, what has your PR message achieved? As you pass others in the hall, what is the first thing they see? How is your PR message working? Are people clear about what you want to contribute? Are people responding to you in a more open way or in a manner that is consistent with how you want to be perceived?

What are some finishing touches you want to add to your PR plan given the real work environment? Is your PR plan succinct and free of jargon? Does it incorporate power words? Increase the likelihood of being considered for projects you want or asked for your ideas and opinions because others know what you *can* contribute. Moving forward, keep your PR message fresh to ensure it reflects your 100 Percent Commitment.

Don't Be a Stranger

You've reconnected and reinforced your network of contacts throughout the company and beyond within a short time frame . . . great job! Today, it's so much easier to call on your network to help you get things done. They want to help you. Keep your network fresh and blossoming.

- Stay connected with people; have lunch with them on a regular basis.
- Build networking time into your calendar and task list.
- Don't be shy about reaching out for help or sharing information.

As part of giving and taking 100 percent, you've made an investment of time and effort, and maybe extended yourself to others in a way that you have not done before. As you continue down the path of success, your relationships will support you the entire way.

JOB SPA BONUS CHALLENGE

Have lunch with three different people this week.

Put It All Together

Congratulations on completing the eleventh week of your Job Spa. You've received a clean bill of Job Spa health! Before you get your hot-stone massage to relax and bask in your accomplishments, let's ensure you put everything into practice.

This week you've taken a look at your Job Spa skills, done a thorough review of the skills you've developed, and accepted a few action items to keep you on your toes. You've come a long way, baby! This also serves to remind you to keep up the skills; they are the gateway to continuing on your 100 Percent Commitment path.

Here is your calendar for the week. Plug in what you need to do in Week Eleven to get your reflections and ideas into action.

Before you get ready for a well-deserved weekend, think back on the week. What went well? What did you learn? What do you want to work on or accomplish next week?

Congratulations on completing your eleventh Job Spa week!

JOB SPA TREAT for the WEEK

Go to your favorite inspirational place (e.g., beach, museum, or the countryside).

Calendar for Week (11) Day (1) 2 3 4 5

Time	Action	Notes
6:00 A.M.		
7:00 A.M.		
8:00 A.M.		
9:00 A.M.		
10:00 A.M.		
11:00 A.M.		
12:00 P.M.		
1:00 P.M.		
2:00 P.M.		
3:00 P.M.		
4:00 P.M.		
5:00 P.M.		
6:00 P.M.		
7:00 P.M.		

REMINDERS

- Keep practicing the skills you've learned from *Job Spa*!
- Confirm your boundaries and priorities.
- Coach someone.
- Remove jargon from your PR plan.

Calendar for Week (11) Day 1 (2) 3 4 5

Time	Action	Notes
6:00 A.M.		
7:00 A.M.		
8:00 A.M.		
9:00 A.M.		
10:00 A.M.		
11:00 A.M.		
12:00 P.M.		
1:00 P.M.		
2:00 P.M.		
3:00 P.M.		
4:00 P.M.		
5:00 P.M.		
6:00 P.M.		
7:00 P.M.		

Calendar for Week (11) Day 1 2 (3) 4 5

Time	*Action*	*Notes*
6:00 A.M.		
7:00 A.M.		
8:00 A.M.		
9:00 A.M.		
10:00 A.M.		
11:00 A.M.		
12:00 P.M.		
1:00 P.M.		
2:00 P.M.		
3:00 P.M.		
4:00 P.M.		
5:00 P.M.		
6:00 P.M.		
7:00 P.M.		

Calendar for Week (11) Day 1 2 3 (4) 5

Time	Action	Notes
6:00 A.M.		
7:00 A.M.		
8:00 A.M.		
9:00 A.M.		
10:00 A.M.		
11:00 A.M.		
12:00 P.M.		
1:00 P.M.		
2:00 P.M.		
3:00 P.M.		
4:00 P.M.		
5:00 P.M.		
6:00 P.M.		
7:00 P.M.		

Calendar for Week (11) Day 1 2 3 4 (5)

Time	Action	Notes
6:00 A.M.		
7:00 A.M.		
8:00 A.M.		
9:00 A.M.		
10:00 A.M.		
11:00 A.M.		
12:00 P.M.		
1:00 P.M.		
2:00 P.M.		
3:00 P.M.		
4:00 P.M.		
5:00 P.M.		
6:00 P.M.		
7:00 P.M.		

week twelve
LOOK AHEAD

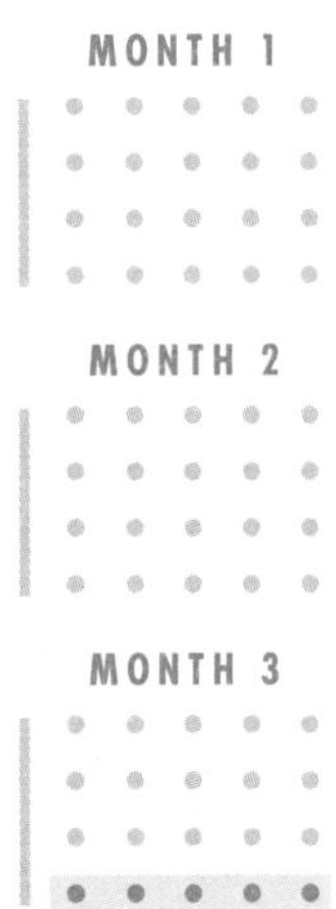

"I'm wrapping up my Job Spa treatment. Twelve weeks ago I was floating along . . . not happy, not feeling bad, just kinda 'there.' Now I have options, and I see my current company and job in a different light. That said, there are still challenges: politics, difficult coworkers, and things in this company that don't make sense. However, I can deal with the issues because I have the skills and the right perspective.

"Over the past twelve weeks I have gotten more done than I ever have at my job. This has been an incredibly valuable process that has helped me define what I want to achieve for myself and contribute to my company. I feel like there is equity between what I am giving and taking. I feel refreshed. I have taken the time to learn more about my company, reconnected with coworkers I haven't talked to in months, and met coworkers who are not just valuable to my job but are really interesting people.

"I have taken accountability for my success. As a result, the most valuable realization I have made is that I have opportunities for growth in both my profession and career. With so many choices, I need to think about and focus on what I want for my future."

Welcome to Week Twelve!

Congratulations! You have reached Week Twelve of your Job Spa. My, how time has flown! Prior to Job Spa, you might've thought professional reinvigoration was simply a fantasy! The past three months have ranged from challenging to a time of rediscovery. Most important, it's been your time to restore balance and understand what you want from your work.

You've spent the past three months building a foundation of career vitality and professional success. A true Job Spa is more than just an event. It's a lifestyle. In keeping with your newfound Job Spa lifestyle, spend this last week identifying how to continue to reinforce your success. This is where all that pampering, massaging, training, and exercise pays off. It's time for the ultimate Job Spa treatment: Set a one-year goal.

WEEK 12	JOB SPA REGIMEN: SET A ONE-YEAR GOAL
GOALS	Determine your one-year goal.
TIME	Create a plan with a specific time line.
KNOWLEDGE	Determine the knowledge and skills you will need.
TEAM	Determine the collaboration and coaching you need to do to reach your goal.
IMAGE	Determine how you will use your communication skills, networking skills, and personal PR message to reach your goal.

Goal

You are now a pro at creating effective goals! Like any professional, the test of how good you are is to take your skills to the next level. It's time for the Job Spa challenge! Create a one-year goal. Your goal will help you continue to apply the skills you've learned over the past three months. If you thought that it was time to say *adios* and get back to your old habits, not so fast! If you make the choice to wake up and go to work, you can make the choice to give and take

100 percent. You deserve everything that's possible. It's time to raise the bar and create your bright future!

Your Life in 70mm

When you want to see a movie on a really big movie screen, you look for films that are shown in 70mm as opposed to 35mm. In the same manner, you need to see your life in a big way. We're talking "big picture." Your life is the "big picture," and a one-year goal is about progress in your life. You have the potential to achieve anything you set your mind to. You know from your successes with this *Job Spa* book that it takes focus, dedication, and even a bit of hard work. The exciting and wonderful thing is that you have the know-how and skills to set a goal and reach it. Setting a one-year goal is a powerful way to broaden your 100 Percent Commitment.

Setting and achieving your one-year goal is a big deal. Consider what is important to you? What is going to compel you enough to make progress and stay focused despite the challenges and distractions that emerge? To begin identifying your one-year goal, consider the following questions:

- Where do you see yourself one year from now?
- What you would find rewarding to accomplish in one year's time?
- What do you want to be responsible for creating in your job?
- What do you want your professional legacy to be?
- Is there anything you want to build from your original Job Spa goals?

As you ponder your objective, consider the realities of your work environment and what you've been able to accomplish in the past three months. As you think about what you want to achieve, balance the realities of what is possible and push the boundaries. Don't just make it an easy goal to achieve. It must have meaning to you and push you to bring out the best of your talents.

The Secret Formula

As a seasoned goal-setter, you know that once you set your sights on something, it's time to make sure you set yourself up for success. As with setting goals for either a project or your Job Spa objectives, your one-year goal is no different. It's just bigger and will require a few additional steps and, of course, patience and perseverance.

Make sure your goals are achievable:

- Write it down.
- Ensure it bears the elements of effective goal-setting: positively stated, in your control, clearly defined, and a manageable size so that you can accomplish it in one year.
- Define success (what will it look, sound, and feel like).
- Break your goals down to achievable milestones.
- Identify critical resources and dependencies.
- Then identify time frames and dates for each of your milestones.

You are on your way to a satisfying and effective one-year goal! The purpose of this exercise is to ensure you keep the momentum of your new attitude. Apply your learning to your one-year goal to make sure it remains tangible. Keep your Job Spa muscles lean and toned!

JOB SPA BONUS CHALLENGE

Identify a one-year goal that inspires you to continue to give and take 100 percent.

Time

As you set your sights on your future, particularly the next twelve months, it will be more important than ever to continue to apply and consistently develop your time-management skills. As you create your time line, note which things can be integrated into your role and responsibilities and which will require extracurricular time.

The List

Now you've outlined your milestones and attached some dates. The key to managing your time begins with how you allocate your time to various tasks and milestones. Is your timeline too aggressive or not aggressive enough? Did you account for your time and other people's time? What about other interruptions or priorities?

Once you've attached realistic deadlines, create a task list for each of the milestones. That way you have a focused to-do list at all times, whether your goal requires you to focus more diligently on your current projects or on extra activities. This is your opportunity to continue to put into practice what you've learned over the past three months and put the pedal to the metal!

JOB SPA BONUS CHALLENGE

Identify when you want to accomplish at least three key milestones of your goal.

Knowledge

The wisdom, knowledge, and information from a variety of people around you will play a valuable part in successfully achieving your one-year goal. As part of your fantastic goal, take a closer look at the knowledge resources you will need and when you'll need them. This will help you make sure you have the equipment to sail into the sunset.

If a Barnacle Can Do It

Scientists exploring life in the deepest ocean have discovered that marine invertebrates will adapt and change behavior based upon their environment. Wow, a barnacle that has coping mechanisms! As you think about where you want to be a year from now, what does that mean in terms of the skills you need and don't yet have? What do you need to effectively adapt?

We know that you're just fine the way you are, but just think of the possibilities if you got even savvier in a particular area. What would be most helpful to learn this year to get you to where you want to be at the end of that one-year horizon? Allow yourself to imagine what you can accomplish.

It Might Be Contagious

The most valuable sources of knowledge and information come from the people around you. Whether through casual conversations or a more formal mentoring process, the value of what others know will continue to be a critical resource as you progress toward your one-year goal. As you begin to think through what it takes to accomplish your one-year goal, who in your network will play a part in your success? What about the people who need to be in your network who will make a difference? What steps can you take to begin to make them a part of your network? Keep your Job Spa immune system boosted with a regular shot of knowledge.

JOB SPA BONUS CHALLENGE

Ask three friends to introduce you to three new people who can help you.

You've heard us repeat over and over again (*ad nauseam*) that being a team player is one of the keys to your Job Spa success. Even when your Job Spa is over, the glow of reading this book will live on through your collaboration and coaching of others.

Collaboration

Your collaboration skills are extremely important to maintain. You'd be amazed how many people quickly drop the ball when it comes to collaborating. The way a double-fudge brownie distracts you from your diet, turf wars, egos the size of a football field, and lack of patience can distract you from collaboration. Yes, the contemporary workplace may not always look like utopia, and at times you may feel like an exhausted salmon braving the rapids. But do not give up! Continue to lead by example. You've built such a wonderful foundation with your teammates and coworkers, and just like any garden, it takes maintenance and well, a bit of fertilizer . . . hmm actually, nutrients to keep things beautiful.

Don't go it alone. As you look at your one-year goal, think about whom you want to involve in your effort. Consider which trusted coworkers or identified experts would have valuable insight. The earlier you involve others and make them a part of your objectives, the higher the likelihood they will support you because they have been involved from the beginning.

Coach

While it's important that you continue to help others through coaching, it is also important that you seek coaching to get your game to the next level. You've spent time helping others over the past three months. Now's a great time to ask for some coaching help to figure out what other factors play into your one-year goal that you may not have considered. Just as you don't have to have all the answers when you coach someone else on your team, your colleagues don't necessarily have to have the answers to your questions. They just have to be good at hearing you out and asking good questions to make sure you don't leave any rocks unturned.

As you take a look at your one-year goal, think about a good person inside or outside your team to approach for coaching and mentoring. Conversely, is there anyone you could collaborate with and bring into your one-year goal to help him learn? Sharing the path to your one-year goal can be an opportunity for someone else to learn and grow. Corporate karma has a funny way of catching up with everyone. Build your Corporate Karma Account by identifying others with whom you can share your goals.

JOB SPA BONUS CHALLENGE

Identify two people you'll ask to coach you on your one-year goal.

Image

Pay regular visits to your Image Salon. Your image may need to be adjusted as your professional goals change. You have been evolving your image over the weeks to reflect what you want. As you look toward your one-year goal, determine what changes will need to take place. Identify areas of development for your communication, PR, and networking skills. To reach your goal, continue to pay diligent attention to how your image is supporting your goal.

King of Communication

Continue to radiate your Job Spa glow. Coinciding with your one-year goal, keep up your exercise regimen of effective verbal and nonverbal communication skills. It takes discipline to keep your image in prime shape. Set your sights on image skill superstardom:

- What will you have to start, or continue, to do to look and act the part of a superstar?
- What's the impression you want to leave with others?

- What body language and tone of voice will support it?
- How will your active-listening, rapport-building, request-making and asking/informing skills help you achieve your goal?

Your Personal Billboard

Leverage your PR message as another tool to get what you want. What PR message would support you in attaining your goal? How do you want to be viewed by others? Do you need to adjust anything in your current PR plan to accommodate your new goal?

Your Growing Network

Just because you are at the tail end of your Job Spa, it does not mean you stop paying attention to building and reinforcing your network. Your networking skills are crucial to your continued success. The people you know today at your company may not be there one year from now. People leave positions and companies, and they stop returning your phone calls. Don't put all your networking eggs in one basket. Continue to cast your net far and wide! For your one-year goal, think about who else you need to know. Have fun, relax, and enjoy your many future trips to your Image Salon!

JOB SPA BONUS CHALLENGE

Review and refine your PR plan to reflect your one-year goal.

Put It All Together

Now it is time to put words into action . . . and not for the last time either! You will continue to do this for the rest of your career. Congratulations on completing the twelfth week of your Job Spa!

This week you've taken a look at your one-year goal as part of continuing to build on and reinforce your Job Spa skills and 100 Percent Commitment. You've integrated everything you've learned in the past three months and put it toward your future.

Here is your calendar for the week. Plug in what you need to do in Week Twelve to get your reflections and ideas into action.

At the end of the week, think back on this week and the past three months. What went well? What did you learn about yourself? How will you ensure that you hold on to this learning throughout your entire career?

Congratulations on completing your twelfth Job Spa week!

JOB SPA TREAT *for the* WEEK

Buy yourself something as part of your Job Spa graduation present. Make it something you will use for work to remind you of your 100 Percent Commitment (i.e., pen, cardholder, notebook, or new work bag).

Calendar for Week (12) Day (1) 2 3 4 5

Time	*Action*	*Notes*
6:00 A.M.		
7:00 A.M.		
8:00 A.M.		
9:00 A.M.		
10:00 A.M.		
11:00 A.M.		
12:00 P.M.		
1:00 P.M.		
2:00 P.M.		
3:00 P.M.		
4:00 P.M.		
5:00 P.M.		
6:00 P.M.		
7:00 P.M.		

REMINDERS

- Define your one-year goal.
- Keep practicing your Job Spa skills!

Calendar for Week (12) Day 1 (2) 3 4 5

Time	Action	Notes
6:00 A.M.		
7:00 A.M.		
8:00 A.M.		
9:00 A.M.		
10:00 A.M.		
11:00 A.M.		
12:00 P.M.		
1:00 P.M.		
2:00 P.M.		
3:00 P.M.		
4:00 P.M.		
5:00 P.M.		
6:00 P.M.		
7:00 P.M.		

Calendar for **Week** (12) **Day** 1 2 (3) 4 5

Time	*Action*	*Notes*
6:00 A.M.		
7:00 A.M.		
8:00 A.M.		
9:00 A.M.		
10:00 A.M.		
11:00 A.M.		
12:00 P.M.		
1:00 P.M.		
2:00 P.M.		
3:00 P.M.		
4:00 P.M.		
5:00 P.M.		
6:00 P.M.		
7:00 P.M.		

Calendar for Week (12) Day 1 2 3 (4) 5

Time	Action	Notes
6:00 A.M.		
7:00 A.M.		
8:00 A.M.		
9:00 A.M.		
10:00 A.M.		
11:00 A.M.		
12:00 P.M.		
1:00 P.M.		
2:00 P.M.		
3:00 P.M.		
4:00 P.M.		
5:00 P.M.		
6:00 P.M.		
7:00 P.M.		

Calendar for Week (12) Day 1 2 3 4 (5)

Time	Action	Notes
6:00 A.M.		
7:00 A.M.		
8:00 A.M.		
9:00 A.M.		
10:00 A.M.		
11:00 A.M.		
12:00 P.M.		
1:00 P.M.		
2:00 P.M.		
3:00 P.M.		
4:00 P.M.		
5:00 P.M.		
6:00 P.M.		
7:00 P.M.		

conclusion
your career-long 100 percent commitment

Now that you have completed your Job Spa, hold on to the 100 Percent Commitment you made to your success. The importance of this experience is that the average person works for about forty-five years of his or her life; that's most of our lives. You've made the choice to spend twelve weeks out of those forty-five years to reflect on work. By deciding to take a Job Spa, you've been intentional and accountable to your success, rather than relying on randomness and fate. You've derived meaning from work and contributed to work in a way that you can be proud of.

The past three months was a time to experiment with a new attitude and behaviors. You've had a guide and structure to provide practice and discipline.

In this next year, as you hold on to your 100 Percent Commitment, move toward achieving your one-year goal, and keep honing your five Job Spa skills. Don't fall victim again to the three myths. *Be your own champion.*

You have the power to control the choices you make.

1. Always look for opportunities in every situation.
2. Know your strengths and where you contribute value.
3. Know when and how to ask for help.

Best wishes and enjoy the results of 100 Percent Commitment to your success!

INDEX

ABOUT THE AUTHORS

Milo Sindell, M.S. has developed career training and employee integration programs for disabled adults. He has held senior management positions with Applied Signal, Intel, and Sun Microsystems. He lives in San Francisco, CA.

Thuy Sindell, Ph.D. is director for client services and a leadership coach for Mariposa Leadership, Inc., providing coaching services for *Fortune* 100 companies. Recent clients have included Charles Schwab, Cisco, The Gap, and Wells Fargo. She lives in San Francisco, CA.

They are the authors of *Sink or Swim: New Job. New Boss. 12 Weeks to Get It Right.*

Also available from the authors of *Job Spa*

Sink or Swim:

New Job. New Boss.
12 Weeks to Get it Right.

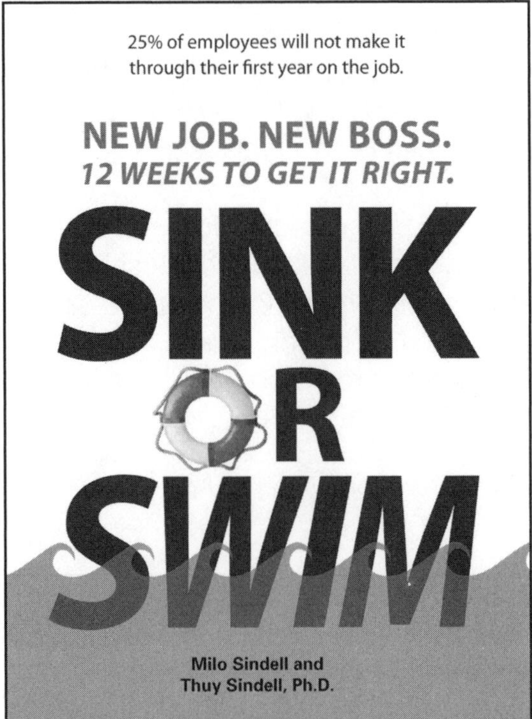

Trade Paperback, $14.95 ($19.95)
ISBN 10: 1-59337-540-9
ISBN 13: 978-1-59337-540-9

"Everyone starting a new job should have this book under their arm at work, next to their plate at dinner, and under their pillow at night."

—Jeffrey Fox, author of the national bestseller, *How to Become CEO*

Available wherever books are sold.
Or call 1-800-258-0929 or visit us at *www.adamsmedia.com*.